CONTENTS

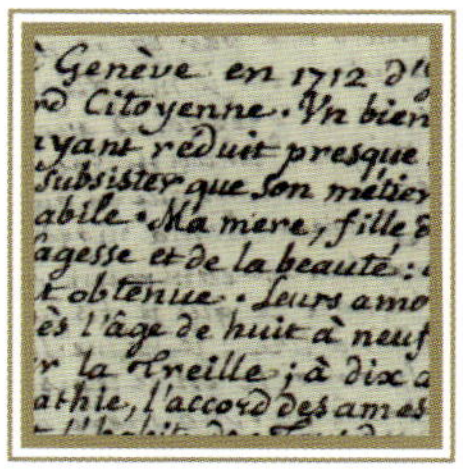

DÉCLARATION
DES DROITS DE L'HOMME ET DU CITOYE
Décrétés par l'Assemblée Nationale dans les Séances des 20, 21, 23, 24 et 26 aout 1789, accepte
ARTICLE PREMIER.
Les hommes naissent et demeurent libres et égaux en droits; les distinctions sociales ne peuvent être fondées que sur l'utilité commune.
II.
Le but de toute association politique est la conservation des droits naturels et imprescriptibles de l'homme; ces droits sont la Liberté, la propriété, la sureté et la résistance à l'oppression.
III.
Le principe de toute souveraineté réside essentiellement dans la Nation; nul corps, nul individu ne peut exercer d'autorité qui n'en émane expressément.
IV.
La Liberté consiste à pouvoir faire tout ce qui ne nuit pas à autrui. Ainsi, l'exercice des droits naturels de chaque hom̃e n'a de bornes que celles qui assurent aux autres membres de la société la jouissance de ces mêmes droits; ces bornes ne peuvent être déterminées que par la Loi.
V.
La Loi n'a le droit de défendre que les actions nuisibles à la société. Tout ce qui n'est pas défendu par la Loi ne peut être empêché, et nul ne peut être contraint à faire ce qu'elle n'ordonne pas.
VI.
La Loi est l'expression de la volonté générale; tous les citoyens ont droit de concourir personnellement, ou par leurs représentans, à sa formation; elle doit être la même pour tous, soit qu'elle protege, soit qu'elle punisse. Tous les citoyens étant égaux à ses yeux sont également admissibles à toutes dignités, places et emplois publics, selon leur capacité, et sans autres distinctions que celles de leurs vertus et de leurs talens.
VII.
Nul homme ne peut être accusé, arrêté, ni détenu que dans les cas déterminés par la Loi, et selon les formes qu'elle a prescrites. Ceux qui sollicitent, expédient, exécutent ou font exécut des ordres arbitraires, doivent être punis; mais t citoyen appelé ou saisi en vertu de la L doit obéir à l'instant; il se rend coupable la résistance.
VIII.
La Loi ne doit établir que des peines stri et évidemment necessaires, et nul ne peut qu'en vertu d'une Loi établie et promulg -eurement au delit, et légalement app
ARTICLE IX.
Tout homme étant présum qu'à ce qu'il ait été déclaré coup jugé indispensable de l'arrêter, to qui ne seroit pas nécessaire pour persoñe doit être sévèrement répr
X.
Nul ne doit être inquiété p même religieuses, pourvu -festation ne trouble pas établi par la Loi.
XI.
La libre communicatio opinions est un des de l'homme; tout cito écrire, imprimer libre de l'abus de cette lib -terminés par la Lo
La garantie de citoyen nécessite force est donc i tous, et non po ceux à qui ell
Pour l'entret les dépenses tion commu être égale -toyens,

The Library, Child of the Revolution

Although the Library of the National Assembly has occupied the magnificent showcase decorated by Eugène Delacroix for over one hundred and fifty years, it came through a turbulent period between the year of its official establishment in 1796 and 1835, the year in which the books were actually displayed there for the first time. The building-up of the collection was, in fact, very closely linked to the institutional development which took place in the years following the Revolution.

THE LIBRARY

At the disposal of the Legislative body

AS OF 1789, the newly established Constituent Assembly sought to conserve its proceedings and also to make available a collection of documents which was representative of the rich knowledge of the period. National Archives were set up in September 1789 and Armand Gaston Camus, M.P. and Secretary of the National Assembly, was elected as their Director. In 1794, a Library, which was common to all the committees of the Convention (1792-1795), (the equivalent of today's standing committees), was set up so as to bring together the scattered documents which had been kept since the Revolution. At the same time, it was decided to draw upon the "literary stores" in which the works confiscated from religious institutions and *émigrés* had been gathered. Thus this first Library inherited twelve thousand volumes for its collection. On 14 ventôse, year IV (March 4, 1796), Armand Gaston Camus, who had now become President of the Council of Five Hundred, had a law passed which "set up a Library at the disposal of the Legislative body". This Library was to be one of the six offices of the Archives of the Republic of which it would shape the destiny and benefit from the notion of legal deposit on account of which one copy of all public publications would figure in its catalogue. In May 1800, a consular decree transferred the management of the National Archives and thus of the Library to the Executive. The archivist was thus appointed and could be dismissed by the First Consul, much to the displeasure of Camus who resigned in 1804, after having been forced to leave the premises occupied by the Library in the *Hôtel de Lassay*. As of 1805, the Library was however "returned" to the Legislative body. The first two librarians - Armand Gaston Camus from 1796 to 1804, and then his first assistant, the Benedictine monk Pierre-Paul Druon from 1804-1833 – are responsible for building up the exceptionally rich collection of the Library. During Camus' time as head of the Library more than six thousand volumes were added to the Library's collection and Druon was to carry out a policy of acquiring rare and precious works helping create a true cabinet of curiosities. As of 1828, the acquisition policy was redirected towards "subjects which more directly involved parliamentary work".

PREVIOUS DOUBLE PAGE
The Declaration of the Rights of Man and of the Citizen
1789, chiseled etching on blue-toned paper by Niquet le Jeune.

ABOVE
Flag of the Parisian National Army
Raymond-Augustin Vieilh de Varenne, 1790.

The Tennis Court Oath

AT THE BEGINNING of the month of May 1789, Louis XVI convened the Estates General in Versailles. Such a meeting had not taken place since 1614. The King was expecting the Estates General to pass fiscal measures which would resolve the financial crisis facing the country. Instead, very quickly the assembly refused the vote by order (Estate) and demanded a limit to the powers of the King. On June 17, 1789, the representatives of the third estate, along with certain members of the clergy, came together as a National Assembly. On June 20, upon the initiative of its President, Jean-Sylvain Bailly, the members took the solemn pledge "to never separate and to meet whenever circumstances required it until the Constitution of the Kingdom be established and laid upon solid foundations". On this document, whose second original is in the National Archives, we can see the signatures of the main actors of the Revolution. One of the two secretaries for this sitting is none other than Armand Gaston Camus, Member of Parliament and first librarian of the Library of the National Assembly.

ABOVE
The Tennis Court Oath
Drawn by C. Monnet, engraved by Helman.

THE HANDWRITTEN MINUTES OF THE SITTING OF JUNE 20, 1789

Among the some six hundred signatories of the Tennis Court Oath, some went on to have outstanding careers, others remained in the shadows, or were guillotined. Robespierre shares the page where he wrote his name with many other astonishing personalities.

ABOVE

The death mask of Mirabeau

On April 22, 1791, the sculptor Houdon made a gift to the National Assembly of the mask of Mirabeau who had died twenty days previously. In the letter enclosed with his donation, the sculptor notes that, having been called half an hour after the death of the M.P., "in order to mould his physiognomy", he got as close "as possible to the likeness".

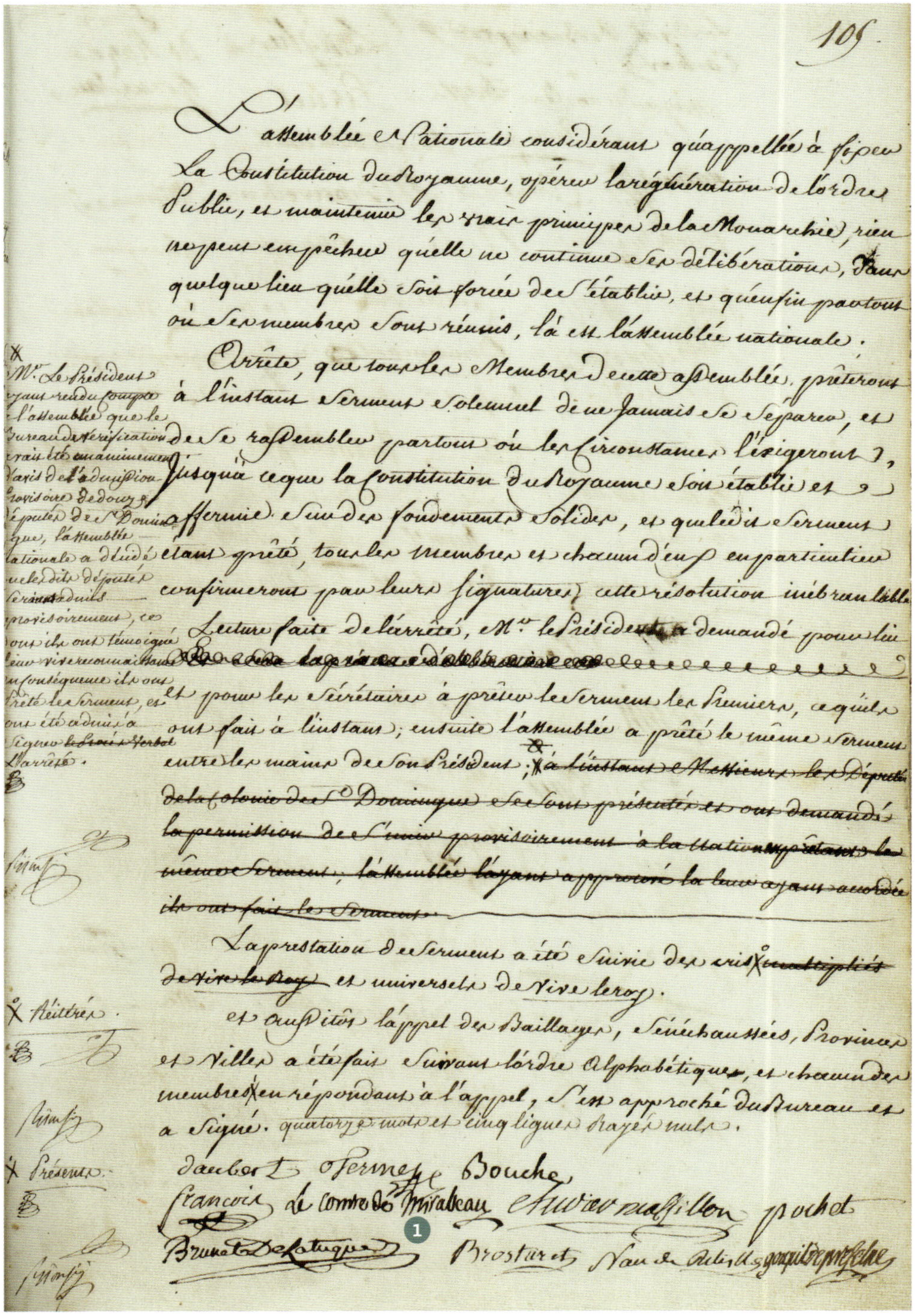

109.

L'assemblée nationale considérant qu'appellée à fixer la Constitution du Royaume, opérer la régénération de l'ordre public, et maintenir les vrais principes de la Monarchie, rien ne peut empêcher qu'elle ne continue ses délibérations, dans quelque lieu qu'elle soit forcée de s'établir, et qu'enfin partout où ses membres sont réunis, là est l'assemblée nationale.

Arrête, que tous les Membres de cette assemblée prêteront à l'instant serment solemnel de ne jamais se séparer, et de se rassembler partout où les circonstances l'exigeront, jusqu'à ce que la constitution du Royaume soit établie et affermie sur des fondements solides, et que ledit serment étant prêté, tous les membres et chacun d'eux en particulier confirmeront par leurs signatures cette résolution inébranlable.

Lecture faite de l'arrêté, Mr le Président a demandé pour lui ~~[illegible]~~ et pour les secrétaires à prêter le serment les premiers, ce qu'ils ont fait à l'instant; ensuite l'assemblée a prêté le même serment entre les mains de son Président; ~~à l'instant Messieurs les Députés de la colonie de St Domingue se sont présentés et ont demandé la permission de s'unir provisoirement à la Nation ayant prêté le même serment, l'assemblée l'ayant approuvé la leur ayant accordé ils ont fait leur serment~~

(margin) Mr le Président ayant rendu compte à l'assemblée que le bureau de vérification avait été unanimement d'avis de l'admission provisoire de douze députés de St Domingue, l'assemblée nationale a décidé que lesdits députés seraient admis provisoirement, en conséquence ils ont prêté le serment et ont été admis à signer ... l'arrêté.

La prestation de serment a été suivie des cris ~~multipliés de vive le Roy~~ et universels de vive le roy.

Et aussitôt l'appel des Baillages, Sénéchaussées, Provinces et Villes a été fait suivant l'ordre alphabétique, et chacun des membres en répondant à l'appel, s'est approché du Bureau et a signé. quatorze mots et cinq lignes rayés nuls.

d'aubert, [illegible], Bouche, François, Le Comte de Mirabeau, [illegible], pochet, Brunet de Latuque, Brostaret, Nau de Belisle, [illegible]

SIGNATURES (PAGES 8 ET 9)

—

1

The Comte de Mirabeau (1749-1791)

Member of Parliament for Aix-en-Provence. During the sitting of June 23, 1789, he concluded his harangue against the Marquis de Dreux-Brézé, the Master of Ceremonies, with the famous phrase : "We shall not leave our places save by the force of bayonets".

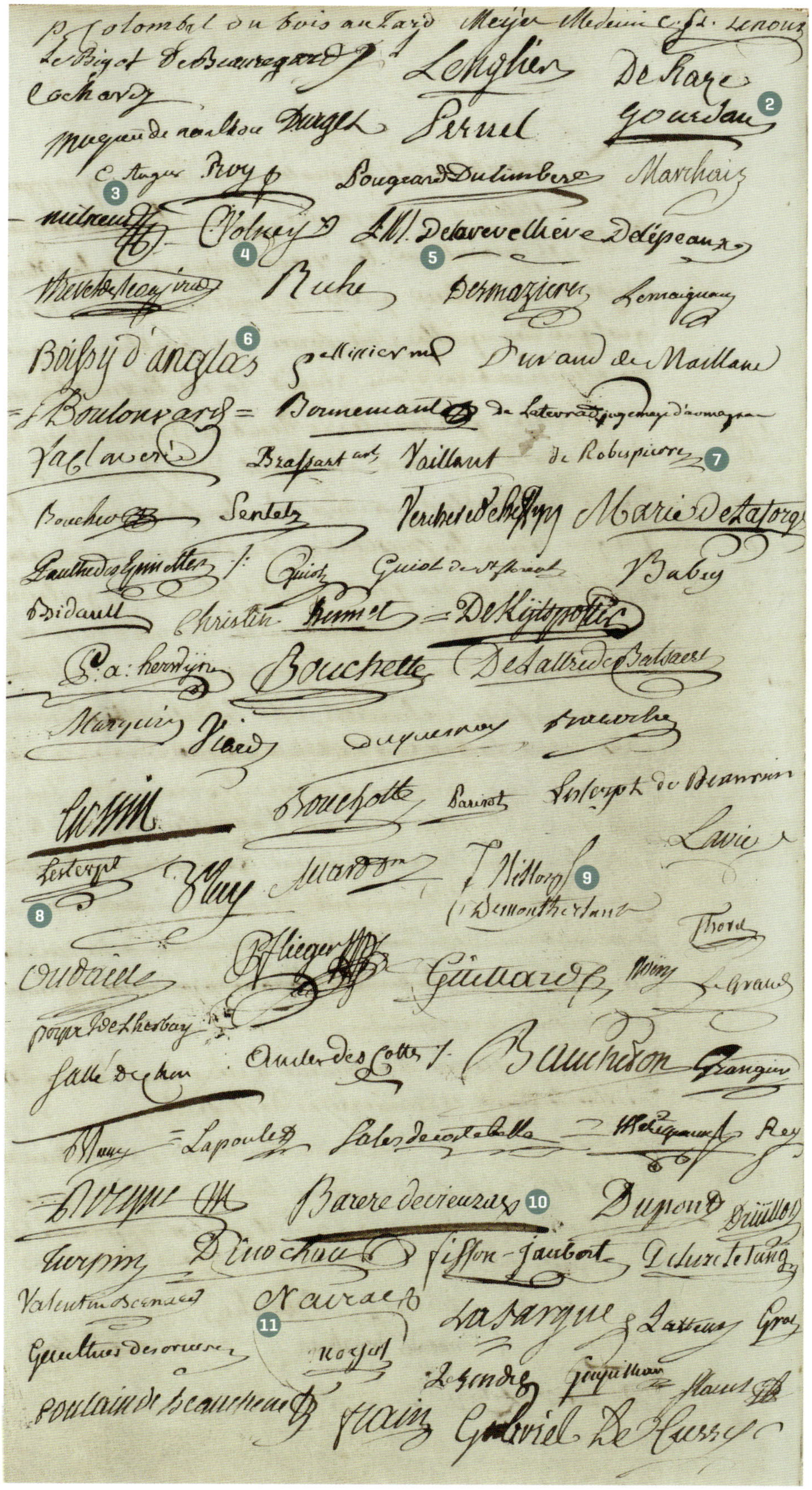

—

2

Charles Claude Christophe Gourdan (1744-1804)

Criminal Lieutenant Assessor in Gray [Haute-Saône], Member of the Third Estate, he voted in favour of the death of Louis XVI and was M.P. until 1798.

—

3

Étienne Jean Augier (1735-1826)

From Cognac, this spirit merchant sat in the National Assembly until September 1791 and defended the prerogatives of the King before leaving politics.

—

4

Volney (1757-1820)

This great history-lover travelled extensively in the East and wrote several books. He was a Member of Parliament in 1789 but was interned during the Terror. He was an enthusiastic supporter of Bonaparte's expedition to Egypt and was later a member of the Senate and a Peer of France.

—

5

Louis Marie de La Révellière-Lépeaux (1753-1824)

Member of the Third Estate representing Anjou, he was elected to the Convention and voted in favour of the death of Louis XVI. He was prosecuted during the Terror, became President of the Directory in 1795 and then a Member of the Institute from which he resigned after having refused to swear loyalty to the Emperor.

—

6

François Antoine de Boissy d'Anglas (1756-1826)

This lawyer of the Parliament of Paris was a defender of the ideas of the Revolution and a Member of the Third Estate for Annonay [Ardèche]. He voted in favour of the banishment of Louis XVI.

—

7

Maximilien de Robespierre (1758-1794)

He was probably the most famous Member of the Third Estate. He was born in Arras and represented Artois, having to borrow ten Louis to pay for the trip to Paris. This lawyer with a great gift for eloquence was to become the influential orator of the Jacobin Club. He was guillotined on 10 thermidor, year II.

—

8

Benoît Lesterpt de Beauvais (1750-1793)

Elected in Dorat [Haute-Vienne], this lawyer, who was close to the Girondins, voted in favour of the execution of the King. He was accused of federalism and of rising up against the Convention and was himself executed in 1793.

—

9

François Millon de Montherlant (1726-1794)

A lawyer at the Parliament of Beauvais and Member of the Third Estate, he was an ancestor of the writer Henri de Montherlant. He was guillotined one month before the end of the Terror for having hosted an *émigré*.

—

10

Bertrand Barère de Vieuzac (1755-1841)

He was a lawyer and a journalist and was, at the beginning the spokesman of the moderate liberals before presiding over the Convention during the trial of Louis XVI and then taking an active part in the Terror.

—

11

Pierre Nairac (1732-1814)

This merchant was elected Member of the Third Estate for Bordeaux, and he sat in the Assembly until 1791.

ROBESPIERRE LAWMAKER

Robespierre and the 1791 Constitutional Bill

THIS COPY of the 1791 Constitutional Bill belonged to Robespierre himself. In preparation for the debate in the Constituent Assembly which was to take place in August 1791, he noted, on this copy, arguments that he intended to use to oppose several points in the text. Maximilien de Robespierre (1758-1794) thus vigorously attacks the selective suffrage system which was introduced by decree in October 1789, on the three levels of being an active citizen, voter and eligible for election. “This decree is a caricature of yourselves. Can those who elected you be stripped by you?” he was to exclaim in the Chamber on August 11, 1791. He was partially listened to on this particular point. Robespierre also reminded the Assembly, in a reference to Jean-Jacques Rousseau, that legislative power, which was a direct result of the sovereignty of the people, could not be delegated and he thus displayed his violent opposition to the role given to the King in the functioning of the institutions: “Be clear about this: it is your committees which have violated the Constitution and it is I who defend it”. This extraordinary manuscript was acquired at an auction in 1989.

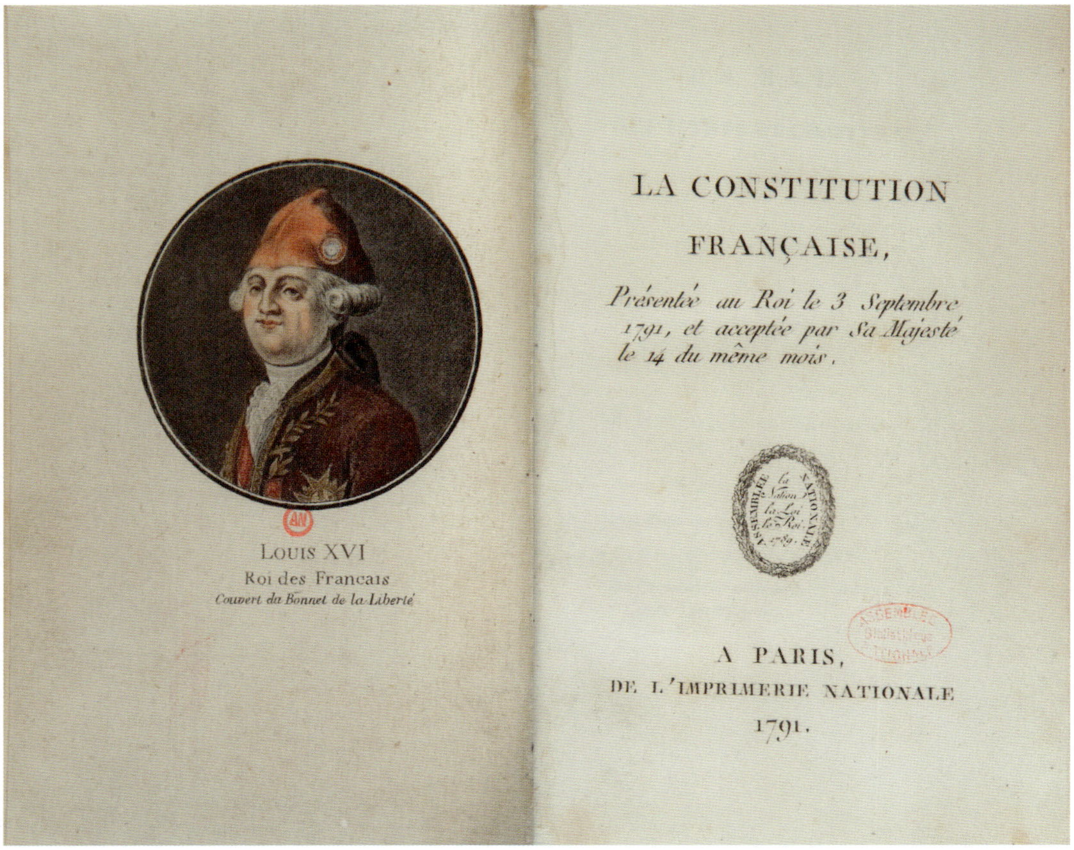

LEFT
The 1791 French Constitution

Paris. National Printshop, in-12, binding in red Moroccan leather.

This Act introduced a constitutional monarchy based on the separation of powers. The sovereign, King of the French, (represented in an inset) had to pledge an oath of fidelity to the Nation.

RIGHT
Constitutional Bill presented to the National Assembly by the Constitution and Revision Committees, 1791

Paris. National Printshop, in-4, half-binding in brown leather, sleeve and case in red Moroccan leather.

++ on fait plus; on aneantit la souveraineté même; car on aucune section du peuple; le peuple s'en attribue l'exercice, quand il dit.

~~inaliénable~~ la nation ne peut ~~exercer~~ les exercer que par delegation.

remarquez bien que ce sont vos comités qui ont violé la constitution et moi qui la defens-

1750, 1

TITRE III.

1750, 1751, 1752, 1753

Des Pouvoirs publics.

ARTICLE PREMIER.

La Souveraineté eſt une, indiviſible, & appartient à la Nation; aucune ſection du peuple ne peut s'en attribuer l'exercice. il n'y a

II.

La Nation, de qui ſeule émanent tous les pouvoirs, ne peut les exercer que par délégation.

La Conſtitution françoiſe eſt repréſentative : les repréſentans ſont le Corps légiſlatif & le Roi.......

III.

Le Pouvoir légiſlatif eſt délégué à une Aſſemblée Nationale compoſée de repréſentans temporaires, librement élus par le peuple, pour être exercé par elle, avec la ſanction du Roi, de la manière qui ſera déterminée ci-après.

IV.

Le gouvernement eſt monarchique : le Pouvoir exécutif eſt délégué au Roi, pour être exercé ſous ſon autorité, par des miniſtres & autres agens reſponſables, de la manière qui ſera déterminée ci-après.

~~la~~ le pouvoir legislatif, le pouvoir judiciaire, le pouvoir executif ~~ne~~ sont des parties du pouvoir souverain, divisé par sous le rapport des divers objets auxquels il s'applique +°

~~si la nation aliénait de quelque manière que~~

+++ remarquez je vous prie que le pouvoir legislatif ne peut être delegué de cette manière car il est l'essence même de la souveraineté. Rousseau il n'y auroit plus aucune l'ombre de la volonté générale; puis que l'on suppose ici que le Roi partage cette délégation du pouvoir legislatif +++

+° le pouvoir doit être bien distingué des fonctions; la nation delegue en effet les diverses fonctions publiques; mais le pouvoir ne peut être aliéné ni délégué. si l'on pouvoit deleguer ces pouvoirs en detail, il s'ensuivroit que la ~~s~~ souveraineté pourroit être ~~alie~~ deleguée; et alors vous adopteriez ce qu'a proposé ~~le comité~~ m. malouet; vous feriez plus; vous decreteriez qu'elle peut être aliénée. car la delegation perpetuelle. ni convention; ni aucun moien pour la nation de reformer les abus du corps legislatif. +++

THE ORIGIN OF THE NATIONAL ANTHEM

The *Marseillaise*

ROUGET DE LISLE (1760-1836) was a Captain in the engineering corps of the Army of the Rhine when war was declared on the eastern front. In 1792, he was given by the Mayor of Strasbourg the mission of composing "a beautiful song for these citizen soldiers who came from all corners in answer to the call of the homeland in danger". This was to become "the Warsong of the Army of the Rhine" which would be taken up by the battalions of soldiers from Marseilles who were called to Paris during the insurrection of August 10, 1792. The decree of 26 messidor, year III (July 24, 1795) set the *Marseillaise* as the national anthem until the First Empire. It took on this status once more in 1879.

BELOW

***Essays in verse and in prose containing the signed manuscript of the Marseillaise,* 1796**

Paris, Didot aîné, in-8.

Copy which was displayed at the Universal Exhibition, 1889.

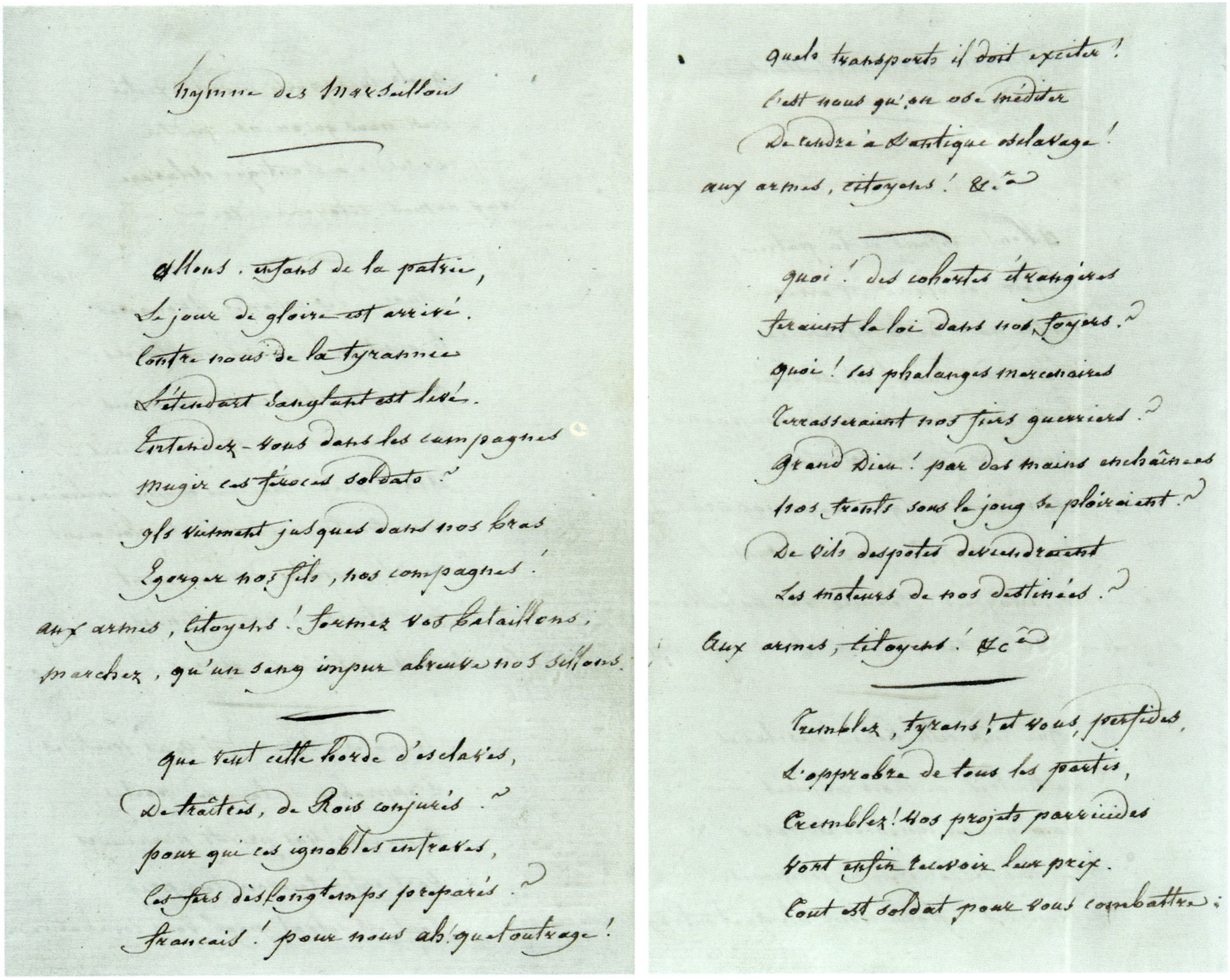

Hymne des Marseillois

Allons, enfans de la patrie,
Le jour de gloire est arrivé.
Contre nous de la tyrannie
L'étendart sanglant est levé.
Entendez-vous dans les campagnes
Mugir ces féroces soldats?
Ils viennent jusques dans nos bras
Egorger nos fils, nos compagnes!
aux armes, citoyens! formez vos bataillons,
marchez, qu'un sang impur abreuve nos sillons.

Que veut cette horde d'esclaves,
De traîtres, de Rois conjurés?
pour qui ces ignobles entraves,
ces fers dès longtemps préparés?
Français! pour nous ah! quel outrage!
quels transports il doit exciter!
C'est nous qu'on ose méditer
De rendre à l'antique esclavage!
aux armes, citoyens! &c.a

quoi! des cohortes étrangères
feraient la loi dans nos foyers?
quoi! ces phalanges mercenaires
Terrasseraient nos fiers guerriers?
Grand Dieu! par des mains enchaînées
nos fronts sous le joug se ploiraient?
De vils despotes deviendraient
Les moteurs de nos destinées?
Aux armes, citoyens! &c.a

Tremblez, tyrans! et vous, perfides,
L'opprobre de tous les partis,
Tremblez! vos projets parricides
Vont enfin recevoir leur prix.
Tout est soldat pour vous combattre;

POSTERS OF THE REVOLUTION

Since 1832 the Library has kept a collection of over two thousand revolutionary posters which were brought together by Louis-François Portiez, M.P. for Oise in the Convention and then in the Council of Five Hundred. They represent a very precious insight into a period when the use of posters as a means of communication was extremely widespread. Amongst these posters one can find the addresses of Olympe de Gouges (1748-1793), a committed woman of letters whose liberty of expression and opposition to Robespierre would lead to the gallows on November 3, 1793. In her "National Pact", the author of the "Declaration of the Rights of Women" and of the famous, "if a woman has the right to take to the gallows, she should also have the right to take the floor", calls for reconciliation between parties.

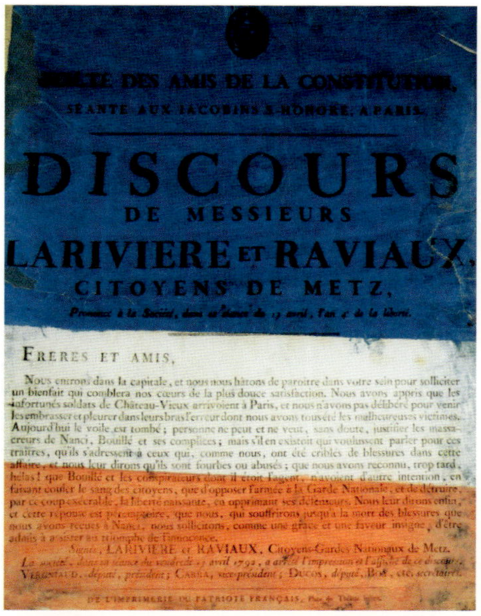

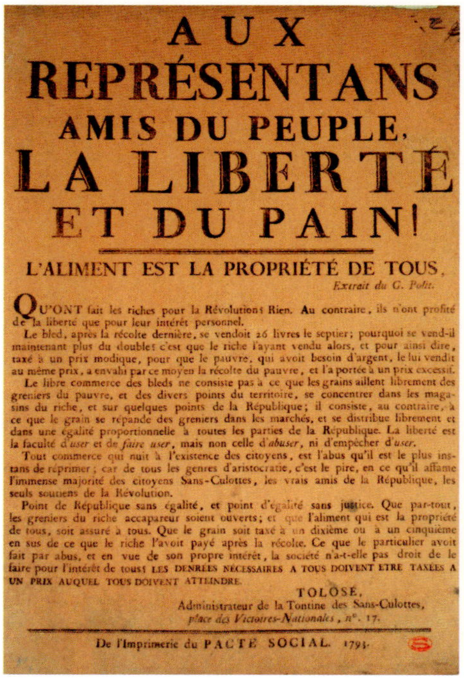

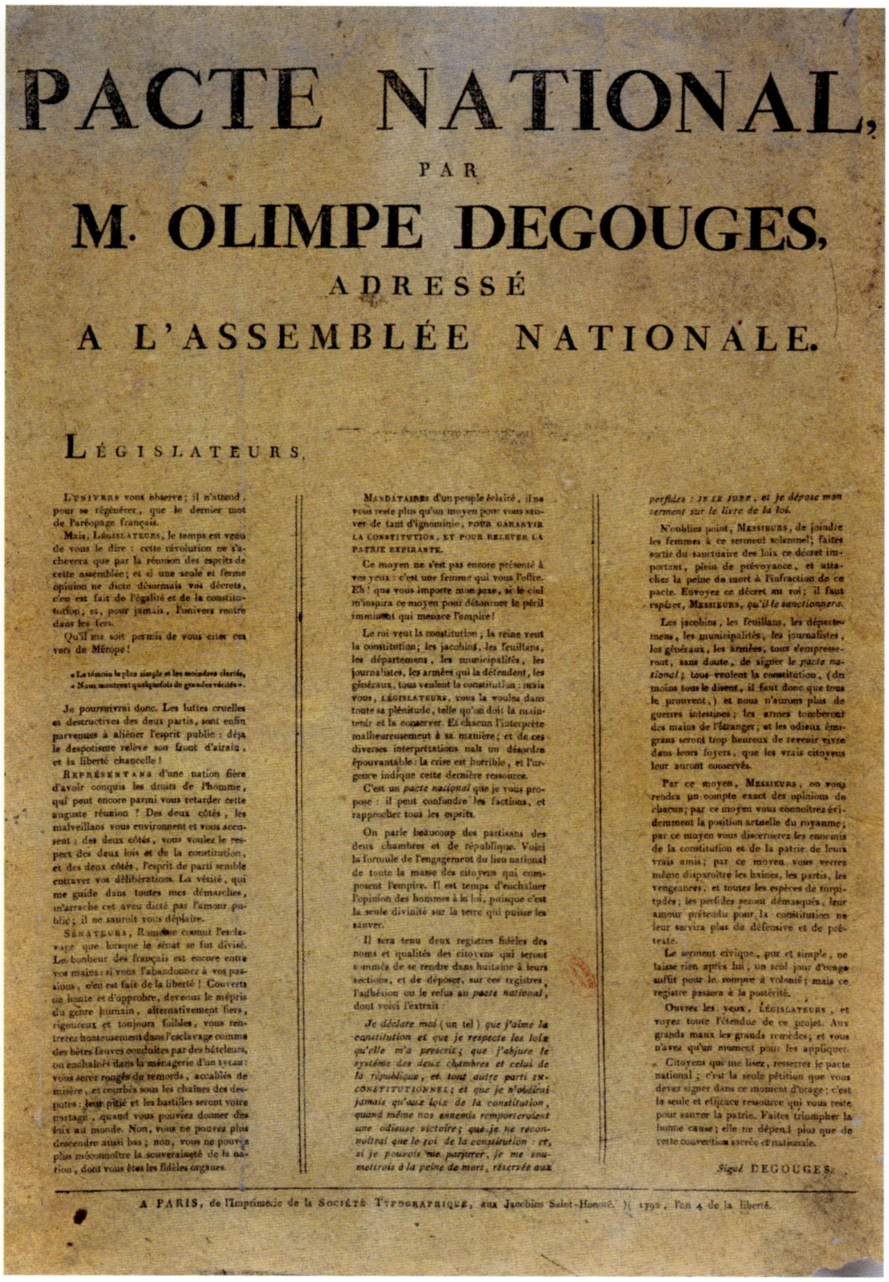

THE SYMBOLIC END OF THE *ANCIEN RÉGIME*

The trial of Louis XVI

THE CONVENTION GAVE over its sittings from January 14-20, 1793 to the trial of Louis XVI. In a very disturbed context, both internally and at France's borders, several questions were put to the Members of the Convention: the first dealt with the guilt of Louis Capet the Members replied positively with an overwhelming majority. The next question concerned the ratification of the judgment of the Convention by the people and in this case the no vote won but by a much slimmer majority. The third question concerning the penalty to be imposed upon Louis Capet was discussed during the sittings of January 16-17, 1793. The replies of the Members of the Convention are extremely varied and those who voted in favour of death sometimes included different types of reprieve. According to the written minutes 387 Members voted for death without conditions, 334 for detention or for conditional death, while 28 were absent or abstained. The question of a possible reprieve was discussed on January 19-20, 1793. There is little mystery concerning the answer and Louis XVI was guillotined the following day.

BELOW LEFT
The trial of Louis XVI
[Detail]
1802. Engraving on colored leather based on a painting by William Miller.
Coll. musée Carnavalet, Paris.

BELOW RIGHT AND OPPOSITE
The manuscript of the minutes of the sittings of January 16-17, 1793
Folios 196 and 234.

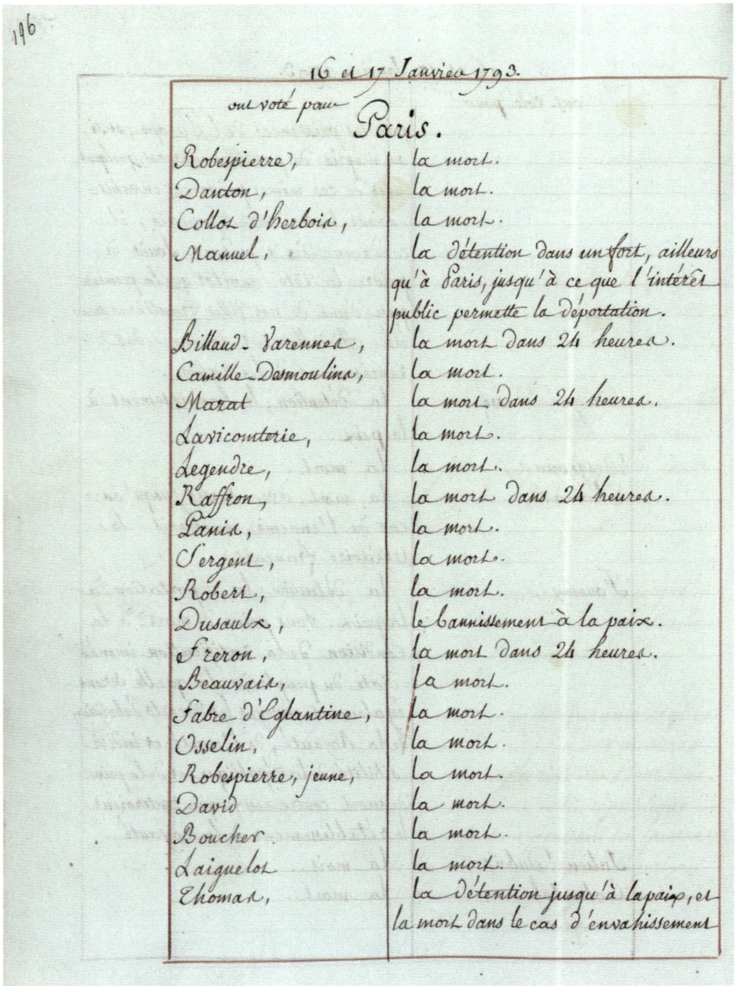

196

16 et 17 Janvier 1793.

ont voté pour

Paris.

Robespierre,	la mort.
Danton,	la mort.
Collot d'herbois,	la mort.
Manuel,	la détention dans un fort, ailleurs qu'à Paris, jusqu'à ce que l'intérêt public permette la déportation.
Billaud-Varennes,	la mort dans 24 heures.
Camille-Desmoulins,	la mort.
Marat	la mort dans 24 heures.
Lavicomterie,	la mort.
Legendre,	la mort.
Raffron,	la mort dans 24 heures.
Panis,	la mort.
Sergent,	la mort.
Robert,	la mort.
Dusaulx,	le bannissement à la paix.
Freron,	la mort dans 24 heures.
Beauvais,	la mort.
Fabre d'Eglantine,	la mort.
Osselin,	la mort.
Robespierre, jeune,	la mort.
David	la mort.
Boucher	la mort.
Laignelot	la mort.
Thomas,	la détention jusqu'à la paix, et la mort dans le cas d'envahissement

234

16 et 17 Janvier 1793.

de l'autre part ... 334.

361 ont voté pour la mort.
26 pour la mort, en demandant une discussion sur le point de savoir s'il conviendroit à l'intérêt public qu'elle fut, ou non différée, et en déclarant leur vœu indépendant de cette demande.

387

Pour la mort sans condition .... 387.
Pour la détention ou la mort conditionnelle 334
Absens ou non votans 28

Total .... 749.

Après la proclamation du scrutin, le Président déclare, au nom de la Convention Nationale, que la peine prononcée contre Louis, est la peine de mort.

Les trois défenseurs de Louis sont introduits à la barre, L'un d'eux obtient la parole et dit : « Citoyens représentans de la Nation. La Loi et votre Décret nous ont

NUMA ET EGERIE
LYCURGUE CONSULTE LA PYTHIE

A unique showcase

With its impressive domes which rise more than fifteen metres above the floor and which were decorated by the great romantic painter Eugène Delacroix, the Library, as soon as it had been finished, was compared to the Sistine Chapel. This magnificent vessel, which is forty-two metres long, is both an architectural exploit and an artistic masterpiece. It took more than fifteen years to be completed and led to many debates.

Delacroix's masterwork

THE *PALAIS BOURBON* became a national palace after the emigration of the Prince de Condé, grandson of the Duchesse de Bourbon. It was given over to the Council of the Five Hundred which first held a meeting there in January 1798. The *Palais Bourbon* and the *Hôtel de Lassay* both definitively became properties of the State in 1827 and 1843. The *Palais* was at that time reconstructed according to the plans of the architect Jules de Joly who imagined the building of a library next to the debating Chamber, so that the representatives of the Nation could have easy access to the documentation necessary for their work. At the beginning of 1835, after four years during which the construction work was interrupted several times and the plans changed, the Library was finally able to take delivery of its emblematic works.

PRECEDING DOUBLE PAGE

The Dome of Legislation
Eugène Delacroix

- Ciceron accuses Verres.
- Numa and Egeria.
- Demosthenes haranguing the waves of the sea.
- Lycurgus consults the Pythia.

LEFT HAND PAGE

The Half-Dome of Peace
Eugène Delacroix

Oil and wax painting.

Orpheus teaching the Greeks the notions of art and civilization.

RIGHT

The Dome of Poetry
Eugène Delacroix

- The Education of Achilles.
- Alexander the Great and the poems of Homer.
- Hesiod and the Muse.
- Ovid with the Barbarians.

After having decorated the new "King's Salon", Eugène Delacroix was commissioned with the decoration of the five Domes and two Half-Domes of the Library. The painter wrote to the then Minister for Trade and Public Works, Adolphe Thiers: "You have given me one of those life-changing opportunities which provide an artist with a whole new career and which should by definition allow him to flourish unless, of course, they do not expose his lack of talent".

In order to accomplish this massive undertaking, Delacroix called upon his pupils. He drew up plans whose guiding principle was to give over each dome to one of the main themes of knowledge: Science, Philosophy, Legislation, Theology and Poetry. Scenes from mythology, the Bible and antiquity were painted on the canvas of the pendants in the workshop and then mounted onto the Domes. The work began in 1838 but had to be interrupted during the sessions

BELOW
Eugène Delacroix
· The Dome of Legislation: inset and preparatory study in black pencil on tracing paper representing Numa and Egeria.
· The Dome of Poetry: inset and preparatory study in graphite on tracing paper representing Ovid with the Barbarians.

ABOVE
The Library of the National Assembly

Overview. Ceiling by Eugène Delacroix, 1838-1847.
Palais-Bourbon.

DAUMIER AND THE CELEBRITIES OF THE *JUSTE-MILIEU*

The entrance lobby to the Library today houses a collection of thirty-two terracotta busts painted by Honoré Daumier (1808-1879) around 1832. These busts represent celebrities of the *juste-milieu*, who were all well-known at the time of the July monarchy. They were commissioned by Charles Philipon in order to serve as models for lithographs published in the satirical magazines *Le Charivari* and *La Caricature*. They were acquired at a public auction in 2004.

FROM LEFT TO RIGHT
André Marie Jean Jacques Dupin, also known as Dupin Aîné (1783-1865)

M.P. for Nièvre and for Sarthe, President of the Chamber of Deputies.

Jacques Lefebvre (1773-1856)

M.P. for Seine, Regent of the Bank of France.

Auguste Hilarion, comte de Kératry (1769-1859)

M.P. for Finistère and for Vendée, Peer of France.

LEFT
Preparatory study in graphite for Attila's horse

Attila, King of the Huns, followed by his hordes of barbarians, destroys Italy and the Arts.

ABOVE AND AT TOP
The Half-Dome of War, Attila

[Overview and detail]
Wax and oil painting.

and operations necessary for the structure. The Minister for Public Works regretted that "the historical paintings in the large rooms and the Library were being carried out so incredibly slowly" and this opinion was shared by the Questeurs, the financial overseers of the Chamber of Deputies, who also were responsible for the management of the site. The two Half-Domes at each end, Orpheus, the bringer of civilization and Attila, the bringer of death, very quickly found their monikers: the Half-Dome of Peace and the Half-Dome of War.

In 1843, a crack appeared in the Orpheus half-dome. In the end, the two Half-Domes were directly painted onto a wax preparation. Talking about the decoration of the half-dome of war, where "Attila, followed by his hordes, tramples upon Italy and the Arts", Delacroix wrote to George Sand: "I'll never be finished with this Attila and his horse". In 1847, towards the end of the year, Delacroix finally invited his friends to see his paintings which had just been finished, nine years after their commissioning. The art historian, Charles Blanc would write this, (Le Temps, May 6, 1881): "Nothing has ever been achieved, in the French school and in terms of frescos, which is more beautiful than this. To imagine such decoration requires a highly elevated mind… and to provide this ensemble with such dignity, with such poise and with the radiance with which it abounds…it needed an exceptional painter, a colourist of the highest degree". Delacroix had also to face criticism and to justify his choices. Nonetheless he could count upon his faithful supporters, notably Adolphe Thiers, who in reply to an M.P. commenting upon the appearance of Attila's horse, stated: "So you have actually seen Attila's horse?". The Library had not seen the end of discussions concerning its decoration and structure. The cracks in the ceiling, due to the foundations meant that, from the very end of the original work, it was necessary to closely keep check on such problems. This is indeed still the case today. In addition, the great conflicts have left their mark upon the building.

THE RAVAGES OF WAR

During the 1870 Franco-Prussian war, the northern half-dome [the Half-Dome of War] was damaged by a shell which created a hole of more than one metre in diameter. In 1914, the idea was considered of setting up a hospital in the Palais Bourbon and the Library was ear-marked to house beds for the wounded: this notion was shelved. At the beginning of the Second World War [as of August 1939], the most precious works of the Library were transferred to premises belonging to the Bank of France in Libourne and were subsequently moved to the Archives of the Department of Puy-de-Dôme. Thus the most extraordinary manuscripts and works of the Library managed to escape the devastation caused by a fire in August 1944 during the combat for the Liberation of Paris. Nonetheless, during this particular event, more than seventeen thousand works, including those dealing with science and theology were destroyed.

ABOVE
The Dome of the Sciences
[First pendant]
Hippocrates refuses the gifts of the King of Persia.

RIGHT
The second floor of the Library after fire damage in August 1944.

IVLIVS CÆSAR
IGNIS
Septentrio
AMERICA
Anno Domini 1492 a Christophoro Columbo nomine Regis Castellæ primum detecta, et ab Americo Vespucio nomen sortita 1499.
AMERICA
SEPTENTRIONALIS
Circulus Arcticus
Fretum Davis
Nova Britannia
Nova Anglia
Nov. Belgium
Virginia
Florida
MARE VIRGINIVM
Frisland
Terra nova
Asores Ins
Al. Flandricæ
MAR DEL NORT
I de Cabo Verde
Tropicus Cancri
MAR DEL ZVR
Circulus Æquinoctialis
OCEANVS PERVVIENSIS
GVIANA
AMERICA MERIDIONALIS
Tropicus Capricorni
MARE PACIFICVM
Rio de la Plata
Fretum Magellanicum
TERRA AVSTRALIS INCOGNITA
Circulus Antarcticus
L.S.
Varias a varijs et antehac editas esse, et quotidie edi tabulas totius Mundi situm depingentes, cuiq; notum est: hac tamen nullam accuratiorem elegantioremq; esse libere dico; quippe quæ succinctius quam omnes aliæ singula depingit, multosque errores aliarum tabular. corrigit. Imprimis vero in Oceano Tartarico et circa illum, multa aliter meliusq; delineat: nec non in nova Guinea, et India Orientali, ut et in America Sept. et Mar del Zur, ac versus Fretum Magellanicum plurima innovat mutatque vale et fruere.
Meridies
GERARDVS MERCATOR Flander
AQVA

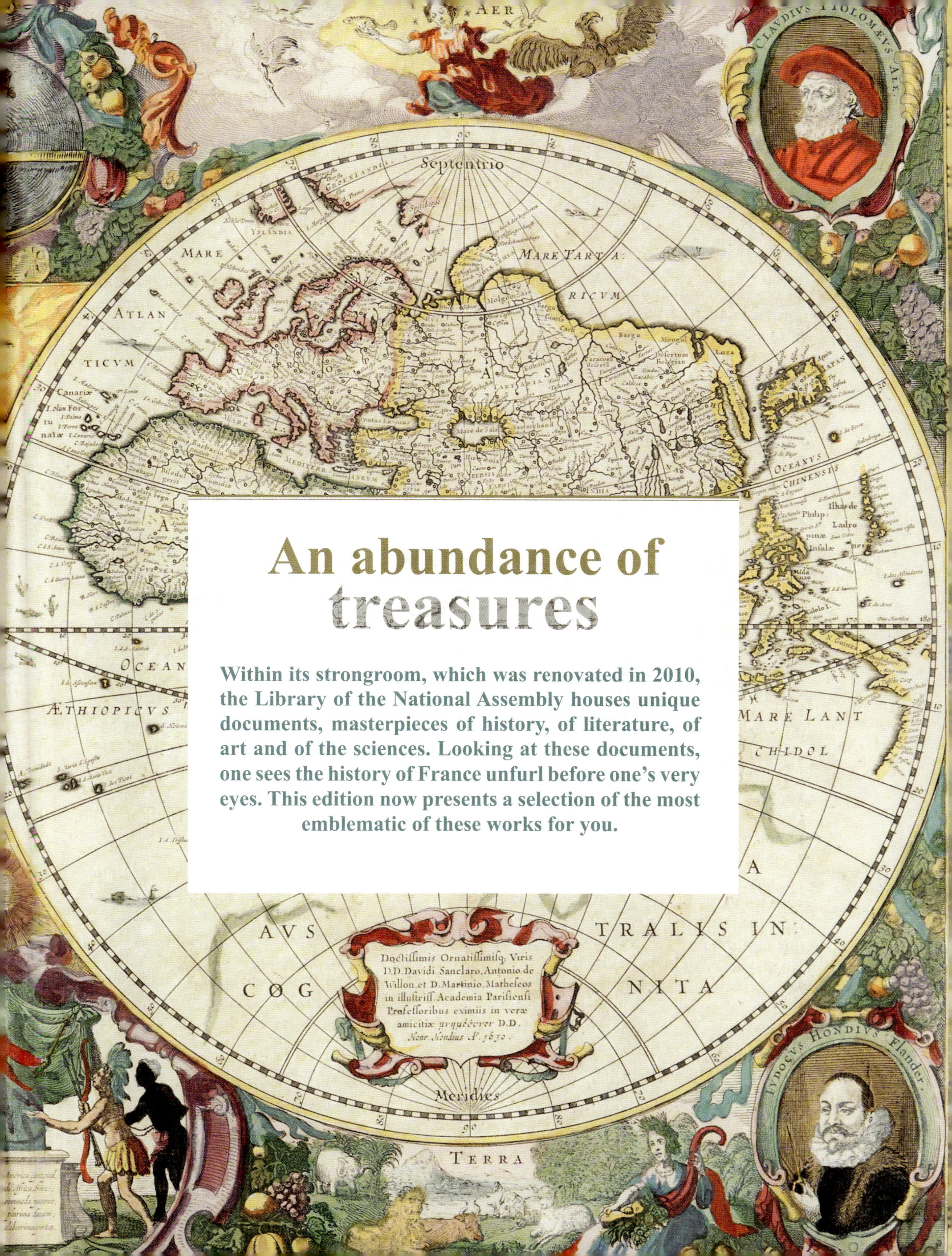

An abundance of treasures

Within its strongroom, which was renovated in 2010, the Library of the National Assembly houses unique documents, masterpieces of history, of literature, of art and of the sciences. Looking at these documents, one sees the history of France unfurl before one's very eyes. This edition now presents a selection of the most emblematic of these works for you.

Treasures
of Theology

بسم الله الرحمن الرحيم
الحمد لله الذي خلق السموت والارض
وجعل الظلمت والنور ثم الذين
كفروا بربهم يعدلون هو الذي
خلقكم من طين ثم قضى اجلا واجل
مسمى عنده ثم انتم تمترون وهو
الله في السموت وفي الارض يعلم سركم

The oldest documents of the Library are two Latin Bibles: the first from the 9th Century and the second from the 12th Century with the arms of a convent of the* Minimes de Chaillot. *The presence of a large number of religious works at the National Assembly can be explained by their origin – the goods belonging to the Church which were nationalized during the Revolution and which came from many different religious congregations. In addition, we must take into account the taste for theology of the first two librarians. The first, Armand Gaston Camus, had been the lawyer for the clergy at the Parliament of Paris. He was an M.P., then President of the Constituent Assembly and subsequently of the Council of the Five Hundred. His successor, Pierre-Paul Druon, was a former Benedictine monk. He was curate to the Legislative body whilst also being librarian.

The Mainz Bible

PRINTED ON UTERINE VELLUM, the finest quality parchment, this volume dating from the earliest days of the history of printing which is an incunabulum, is the work of Fust and Schoeffer, associates of Gutenberg and the purchasers of his printing equipment when he encountered financial difficulties. This Bible, which was printed on forty-eight lines, is the fourth edition after the forty-two line Bibles (the famous Gutenberg Bible which was the first large book ever created and was printed in Mainz with the help of moveable type between 1452 and 1454) and the thirty-six line Bibles. This incunabulum was purchased in 1821 by the second librarian, Druon. Upon his death, he bequeathed his own library to the Chamber of Deputies.

ABOVE AND RIGHT

Biblia latina
or the Mainz Bible
Mainz, Fust et Schoeffer, 1462. Two volumes in-folio on vellum with miniatures.

LEFT HAND PAGE, FROM LEFT TO RIGHT AND TOP TO BOTTOM

Historial Bible
Pierre le Mangeur (Petrus Comestor)
XIVth Century.

Missel from the Abbey of Saint-Claude
XVe–XVIe Centuries.

Latin Bible with the prologues of Saint Jérôme
XIIth Century.

Mainz Bible
XVth Century.

The Book of Hours,* also known as *the Book of Croy
Around 1480.

Fragments from the Koran
XVIIth–XVIIIth Centuries.

PRECEDING DOUBLE PAGE

New Atlas or Theatre of the World
Johannem Janssonium
1657.

MAGNIFICENT ILLUMINATED MANUSCRIPTS

The missal of Saint-Claude

THIS MANUSCRIPT ON PARCHMENT, which was commissioned by an Archbishop, is made up of one hundred and one letters which are decorated with different saints and twenty-three paintings by several illuminators. These scenes represent the Nativity, the adoration by the Magi, Saint Martin, Saint Romain, Saint Lupicin, Saint Benedict as well as Saints Oyend and Claude the founders of the monastery in the Jura region. This manuscript was probably produced in Paris at the very end of the XVth Century and would have been brought back there during the revolutionary period.

Missal from the Abbey of Saint-Claude

xvth-xvith Centuries. Parchment. 236 pages with 2 columns. Modern binding.

BELOW: Saint Martin, Saint Lupicin and Saint Benedict. / RIGHT HAND PAGE: The Tree of Jesse.

Vultum
tuum de
precabū
tur om̄s
diuites
plebis adducentur regi vir
gines post eam proxime ei
adducentur tibi in leticia
et exultatione. Psalm.
Eructauit cor meum ver
bum bonum dico opera
mea regi. Gloria patri
et filio et spiritui sancto.
Sicut erat. Oratio

A DISTINGUISHED ORIGIN

The Book of Hours, also known as the Book of Croÿ

THIS MANUSCRIPT ON VELLUM is decorated with twenty-five miniatures. According to the handwritten annotations at the front of the volume, it would have belonged to Anne de Lorraine, the wife of Philippe de Croÿ. Indeed the coat of arms of this illustrious family, originally from Picardy, can be found on the binding and inside the manuscript. This small collection of prayers for different times of the day was due to be used to follow the different Catholic offices. It was produced in the workshop of a master illuminator in Troyes. The miniatures represent Saint Christopher, David slaying Goliath, and Death riding a bull which corresponded to the prayers of the Office of the Dead.

The Book of Hours, also known as the Book of Croÿ

Around 1480. On vellum, 130 pages. Modern binding in dark-brown Moroccan leather, with the coat of arms of Croÿ.

ilexi quoniam ex
audiet dominus
uocem orationis mee

Masterpieces of different religions

LEFT
Historial Bible
Pierre le Mangeur (Petrus Comestor)

XIVth Century. On vellum, 347 pages with 2 columns, XVIIIth Century, veined calf-binding.

This manuscript belonged to the Cardinal of Retz. It is decorated with golden initial letters and with one hundred and thirty-one miniatures. On one of them *Petrus Comestor* is represented offering his work to the Archbishop of Sens, Guillaume de Champagne. The text reproduces a narrative analysis of the main passages from the Bible, carried out by the theologian *Petrus Comestor*, between 1168 and 1178, and subsequently translated for the first time into French by Guyart des Moulins at the end of the XIIIth Century.

ABOVE

The Apocalypse, Jean Duvet

1561, Lyon. 25 prints on parchment, etched with a chisel, in-folio.

Jean Duvet (1485-1570), who was a very well-known goldsmith and engraver for both King François I and King Henri II, was one of the first French artists to use the process of copper engraving. The prints in this rare book are inspired by the works of Albrecht Dürer (1471-1528).

ABOVE

The Pentateuch in Hebrew

XVIth Century. Parchment roll with two turned-wood rods.

This document which was used for religious offices is more than eighteen metres long and brings together the first five books of the Old Testament. It retraces the history of the Hebrews from their origin up to the death of Moses.

ABOVE

Fragments of the Koran followed by prayers in Arabic and Turkish

XVIIth–XVIIIth Centuries. On paper, 39 pages, Eastern Binding in brown Moroccan leather with gilded motifs.

This manuscript brings together prayers in both Arabic and Turkish which were to be read aloud. It is decorated with a very beautiful cover made up of gold, blue and brown arabesques.

ABOVE

The life of the Apostle Saint James

XIXth Century. Manuscript in the Tamil language, 137 pages bound by a piece of cord.

This manuscript was written in prose with a stylus on leaves made from reed.

Treasures of history

MARAT,
L'AMI DU PEUPLE,
A SES CONCITOYENS.

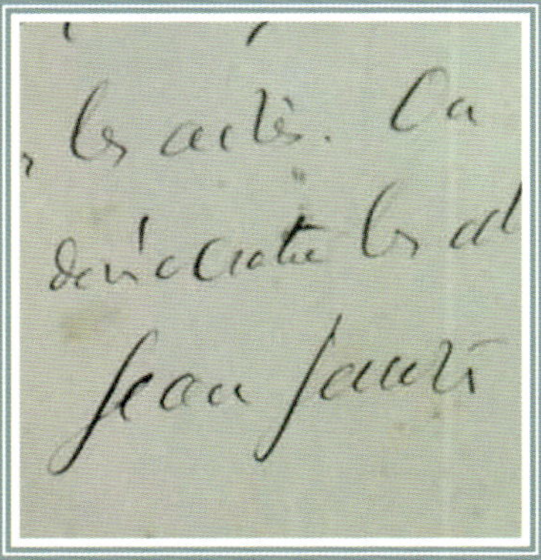

According to the Law of March 4, 1796, the Library of the Legislature was to include a selection of the "most valued" books. Druon, Camus' successor, was responsible for some exceptional and, at times, unexpected, acquisitions. As the "guardian" of the collective political memory, the Library thus also possesses many parliamentary manuscripts.

The "Decades" or the History of Rome by Livy

THE FRENCH TRANSLATION of the "Decades" or "The History of Rome" written by the Roman historian Livy (around 60BC – 17AD) was carried out by the Benedictine monk, Pierre Bersuire, at the request of King Jean le Bon (John II, the Good). It was the first major translation into French of an author from antiquity and thus granted the French language the rank of "language of learning". This manuscript, which is sumptuously illuminated, was presented to Charles VII around 1455. Its first page represents Jean le Bon, the great grandfather of Charles VII in the Great Hall of the *Palais de la Cité* (previously the Parliament), to whom Bersuire, kneeling, presents his translation. This manuscript was acquired by the Chamber of Deputies in 1827.

LEFT HAND PAGE FROM LEFT TO RIGHT AND TOP TO BOTTOM

The "Decades" or the History of Rome by Livy
Around 1455.

Attire of the representatives of the people, Jacques Grasset de Saint Sauveur
1795.

Historial description of Africa
Jean Léon l'Africain
Around 1483-1552. Binding with the coat of arms of Pierre de Mansfeld.

Flag of the National Parisian Army
Raymond-Augustin Vieilh de Varenne, 1790.

Revolutionary poster
1792.

Signed manuscript

Jean Jaurès "Par les oeuvres"
1907.

RIGHT

The "Decades" or the History of Rome by Livy
Around 1455. Manuscript on vellum, 390 pages with 2 columns, 2 large paintings and 29 miniatures. Red Moroccan leather binding with gilded lace.

Prologue du translateur ou livre de la premiere guerre punique que compila maistre leonard de arecio

Tres hault et souverain prince Charles septiesme de ce nom par la divine pourveance roy de france.

THE MANUSCRIPT OF A KING

The second part of the manuscript of the "Decades " is made up of a narrative of the First Punic War by Leonardo Bruni d'Arezzo translated by Jean Lebègue. The first page displays a large miniature which depicts the dedication of Jean Lebègue to King Charles VII as well as two war scenes.

^ The capture of Reggio by the Romans

A group of Romans dressed in armour, attack the town of Reggio and slaughter the inhabitants, fearing that the town might be captured by Pyrrhus, the arch-enemy of Rome.

v The edge of the sword

The soldiers of the Roman Legion are punished for their crimes: they are beheaded on the market square in front of some of the inhabitants of the town.

^ Charles VII and the translator

The historian and Pontifical secretary, Leonardo Bruni d'Arezzo (around 1369-1444) was the author of numerous works including a history of Florence in twelve volumes. His book which was inspired by the Punic Wars and whose translation Jean Lebègue presented to the King, replaced the second of the "Decades" which had been lost.

A HEROINE AND HER JUDGEMENT

The trial of Joan of Arc

ON JANUARY 9, 1431, in Rouen, the trial for "matters of faith" which was to lead Joan of Arc to the stake on May 30, opened before a Church tribunal presided over by the Bishop of Beauvais, Pierre Cauchon. According to the original text which was written in Latin and which no longer exists, five dispatches signed by the court clerks and authenticated by the seals of the President of the Tribunal and by the Deputy Inquisitor, were drawn up. One of these was set down on a parchment certainly for the intention of the President of the Tribunal or for the King of England. This extraordinary manuscript was acquired by Druon in 1811, at the time of the sale of the library belonging to Jules-François de Cotte, President of the Chamber of the Parliament of Paris.

ABOVE
Joan of Arc at the coronation of Charles VII, in the Cathedral of Reims, July 17, 1429
Jean Auguste Dominique Ingres
1854. Oil on canvas, 240 x 178 cm.

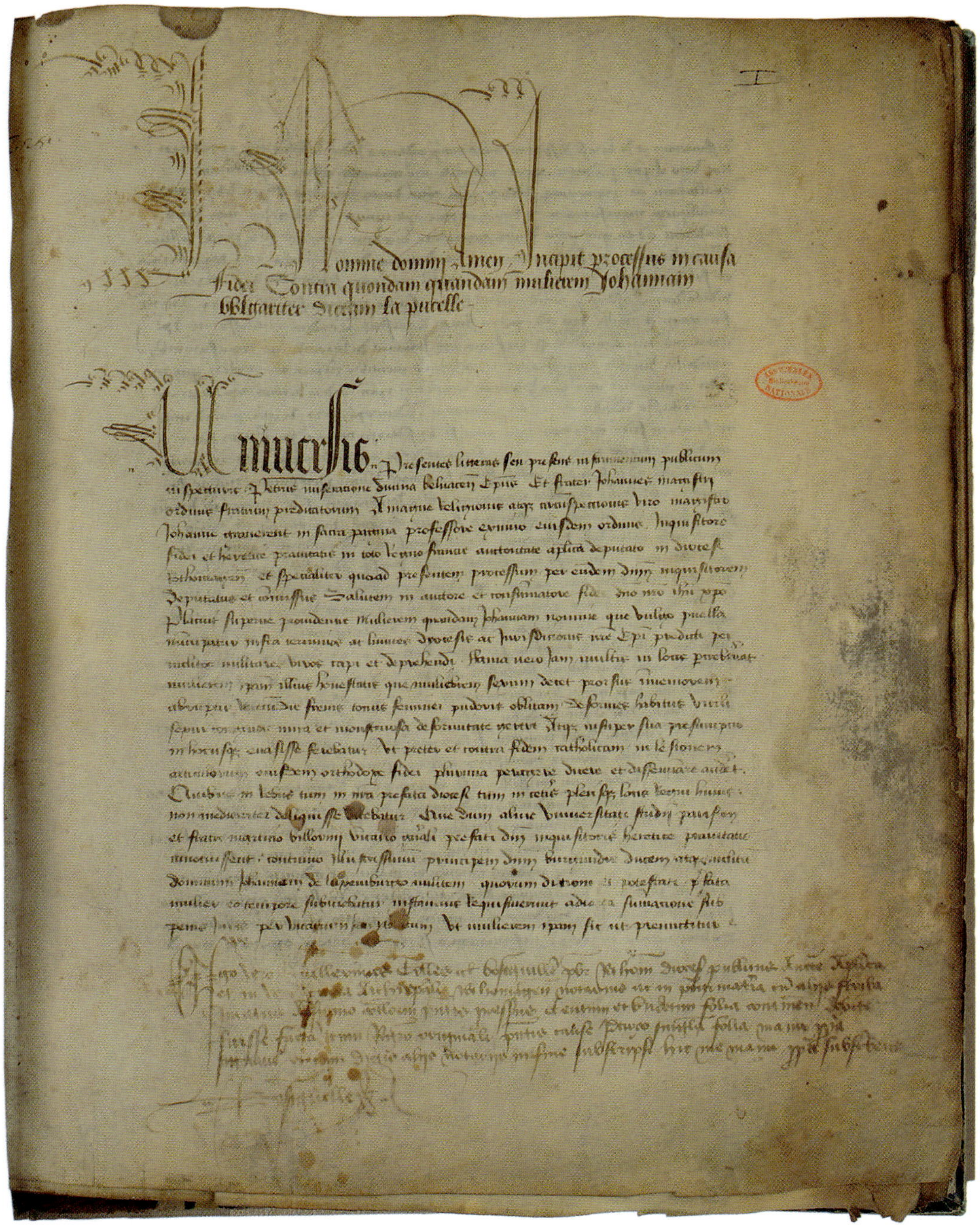

LEFT AND RIGHT
The trial of Joan of Arc
Around 1435. Original dispatch on parchment, 120 pages.

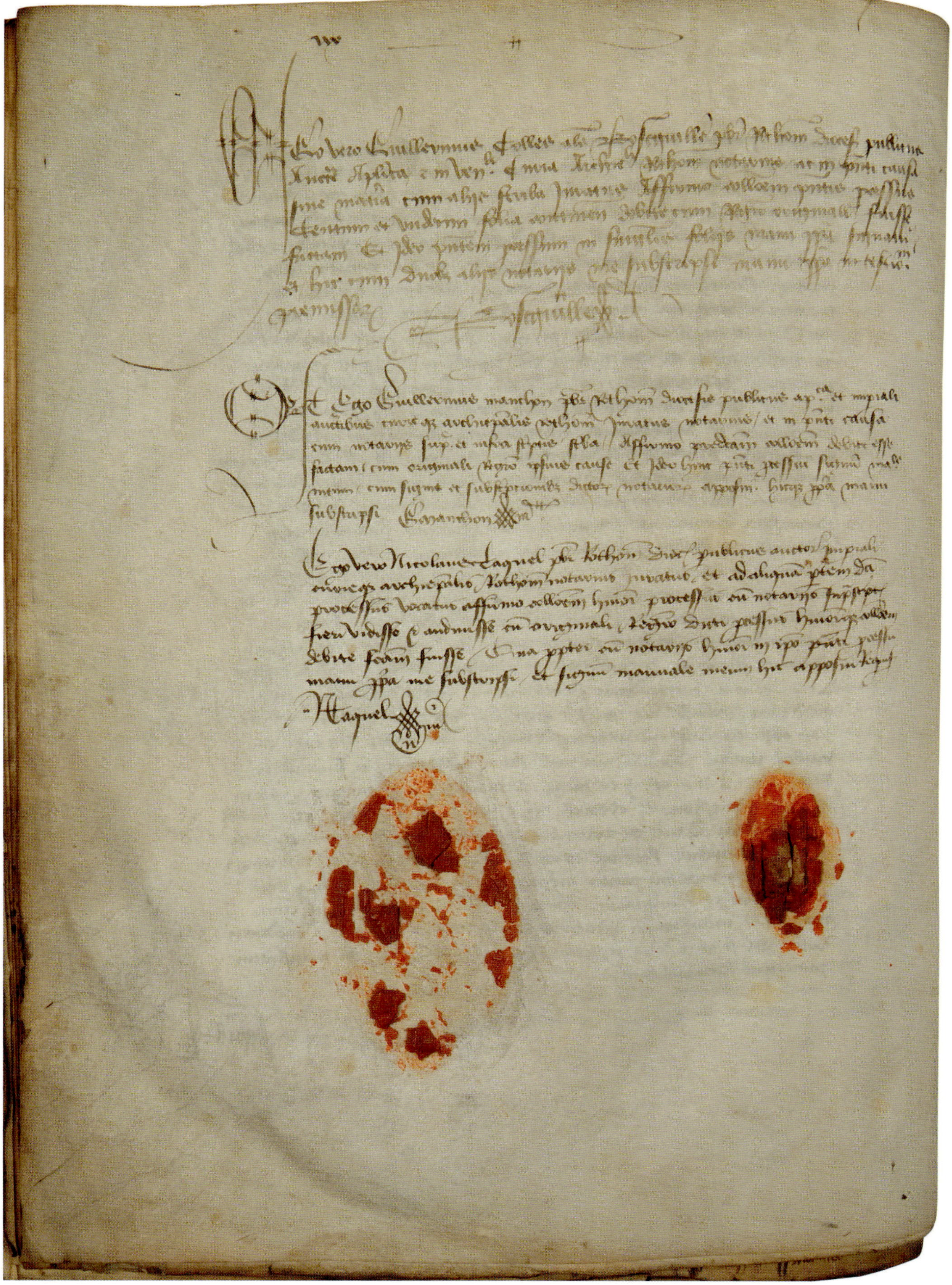

Et ego vero Guillermus Colles alias Boisguillaume presbiter Rothomagensis diocesis publicus auctoritate apostolica et in venerabili curia archiepiscopali Rothomagensi notarius, ac in presenti causa una cum aliis scriba juratus, affirmo collationem presentis processus factam et auditam fuisse cum registro originali, et ideo presentem processum in singulis foliis manu propria signavi, et hic cum dictis aliis notariis me subscripsi manu mea propria [illegible] premissorum.

Boisguillaume

Et ego Guillermus Manchon presbiter Rothomagensis diocesis publicus apostolica et imperiali auctoritatibus curieque archiepiscopalis Rothomagensis juratus notarius, et in presenti causa cum notariis supra et infra scriptis scriba, affirmo predictam collationem debite esse factam cum originali registro ipsius cause, et ideo huic presenti processui signum meum manuale cum signis et subscriptionibus dictorum notariorum apposui, hicque propria manu subscripsi.

G. Manchon

Et ego vero Nicolaus Taquel presbiter Rothomagensis diocesis publicus auctoritate imperiali curieque archiepiscopalis Rothomagensis notarius juratus, et ad aliquam partem dicti processus vocatus, affirmo collationem hujusmodi processus cum notariis suprascriptis fieri vidisse et audivisse cum originali registro dicti processus, hujusmodique collationem debite factam fuisse. Ideo propter cum notariis hujusmodi in isto presenti processu manu propria me subscripsi et signum manuale meum hic apposui requisitus.

N. Taquel

venado
muerte
culebra
dezimo dia
lagartixa
casa
ochavo dia
primero dia
aguila.
tercero dia
sol
quarto dia
pedernal
quinto dia
sexto dia

Codex Borbonicus, a perpetual calendar

THIS AZTEC MANUSCRIPT, made of natural organic fibres, is more than fourteen metres long. It was acquired in 1826 and is outstanding for many reasons: only a very limited number of such religious and divinatory calendars, examples of beliefs which were subsequently prohibited, managed to survive the Spanish conquest; amongst these, this particular example is both the most impressive (thirty-six pages with sides of forty centimetres), with its high quality drawings, as well as being the best conserved example of a codex dating from the pre-Hispanique era, although the accuracy of this dating is still an on-going debate in the scientific community. This calendar which is named after the place where it is conserved, the *Palais Bourbon*, has two major sequences: the first represents the Mexican century of fifty-two years, each of which has two hundred and sixty days divided up into twenty weeks of thirteen days. The second describes the ritual festivals amongst which figures the famous Ceremony of the New Fire which marks the change between two centuries.

LEFT HAND PAGE
Codex Borbonicus
xvth Century.
Aztec Manuscript.
The Goddess of vegetation, Xochiquetzal, wearing her feathered headdress and singing, presides over the destiny of the nineteenth week of thirteen days of the Aztec calendar.

ON-GOING INVESTIGATIONS

The extreme rarity of this manuscript and the questions which remain regarding its origin, its date of creation, its make-up and its fragility, led to the launching in 2014, by the National Assembly and the French Foundation for Sciences and Heritage, of a groundbreaking scientific experience. Under the stewardship of the French Research Centre for the Conservation of Collections (CRCC) – the scientific unit of the National Museum of History which brings together the French National Centre for Scientific Research and the Ministry of Culture – this study calls upon the most recent analytical technologies to characterize in situ the specific components and their breakdown, in particular thanks to hyperspectral imaging. The *Codex Borbonicus* will certainly thus provide us with some of its secrets.

UNDERSTANDING AZTEC TIME

1

2

3

ABOVE RIGHT
Codex Borbonicus
xv[th] Century.
Aztec manuscript.
Fifth week of thirteen days.

LEFT HAND PAGE
Codex Borbonicus
xv[th] Century.
Aztec manuscript.

1. A powerful divinity

A divinity is represented at the centre of each page of the calendar. Each week of thirteen days is placed under the protection of its own divinity. Here, Chalchiuhtlicue, the Goddess of inland and coastal waters presides over the fifth week of thirteen days. She is seated on a throne from which springs a stream in which a man and a woman are carried away by the current. In front of the Goddess one can see containers for sacrificial use.

2. Lines of a divinatory nature

The two hundred and sixty days set out in the ritual or divinatory calendar which make up the first part of the *Codex Borbonicus*, are composed of twenty "weeks" of thirteen days. The days of each week are represented by symbols, all of which are different, in squares which are outlined in red and which are supposed to be read from the bottom of the page on the left to the top of the page on the right.

3. An Aztec day

The twenty signs which follow each other in an unchanging pattern and which are linked to thirteen numbers, create a succession of daily symbols. The signs represent an animal, vegetal or a religious symbol. Each sign is accompanied by a number which is portrayed, just as with an abacus, by one to thirteen red beads. The patrons of the day, represented by birds, occupy the adjacent squares.

THREE MAJOR SCENES

LEFT HAND PAGE

A God in a Man's skin

Xipe Topec, God of skinning and of Spring, presides over the fourteenth week of thirteen days along with Quetzalcoatl, the God of the wind who is represented by a feathered serpent devouring its human prey. Xipe Topec, with a plumed headdress, is wearing a human skin and carries a shield, a flag and a bone. He symbolizes the "new skin" taken on by the earth upon the arrival of Spring.

ABOVE RIGHT

The first human couple

Cipactonal and his wife Oxomoco, the first human couple, are shown on a patio from which a stream flows. They are surrounded by chronological symbols representing twenty-six years and several divinities. The two are old and observe certain rituals: Cipactonal, holds an incense burner whilst Oxomoco spreads grains of corn. They are preparing a divinatory calendar.

BELOW RIGHT

The new fire

The transition from one period of fifty-two years to the next was the moment for a very important ritual festival: the priests gathered at the Temple of Huizilopochtli where a fire was lit in the chest of a sacrificed person. Four priests carried the torches containing the new fire whilst other priests took the fire and brought it to their districts.

The great parliamentary voices

From its very creation, the Library placed enormous importance upon the history of the institution and upon political works. Montesquieu, Condorcet and Bailly were all witnesses to the flourishing political life of the XVIIIth Century. But, in addition, the Library also tells the tales of the significant moments of parliamentary eloquence and allows the voices of the great orators of the Chamber to resonate to our very day. It thus possesses several manuscripts by Lamartine, Victor Hugo, Clemenceau and Jean Jaurès.

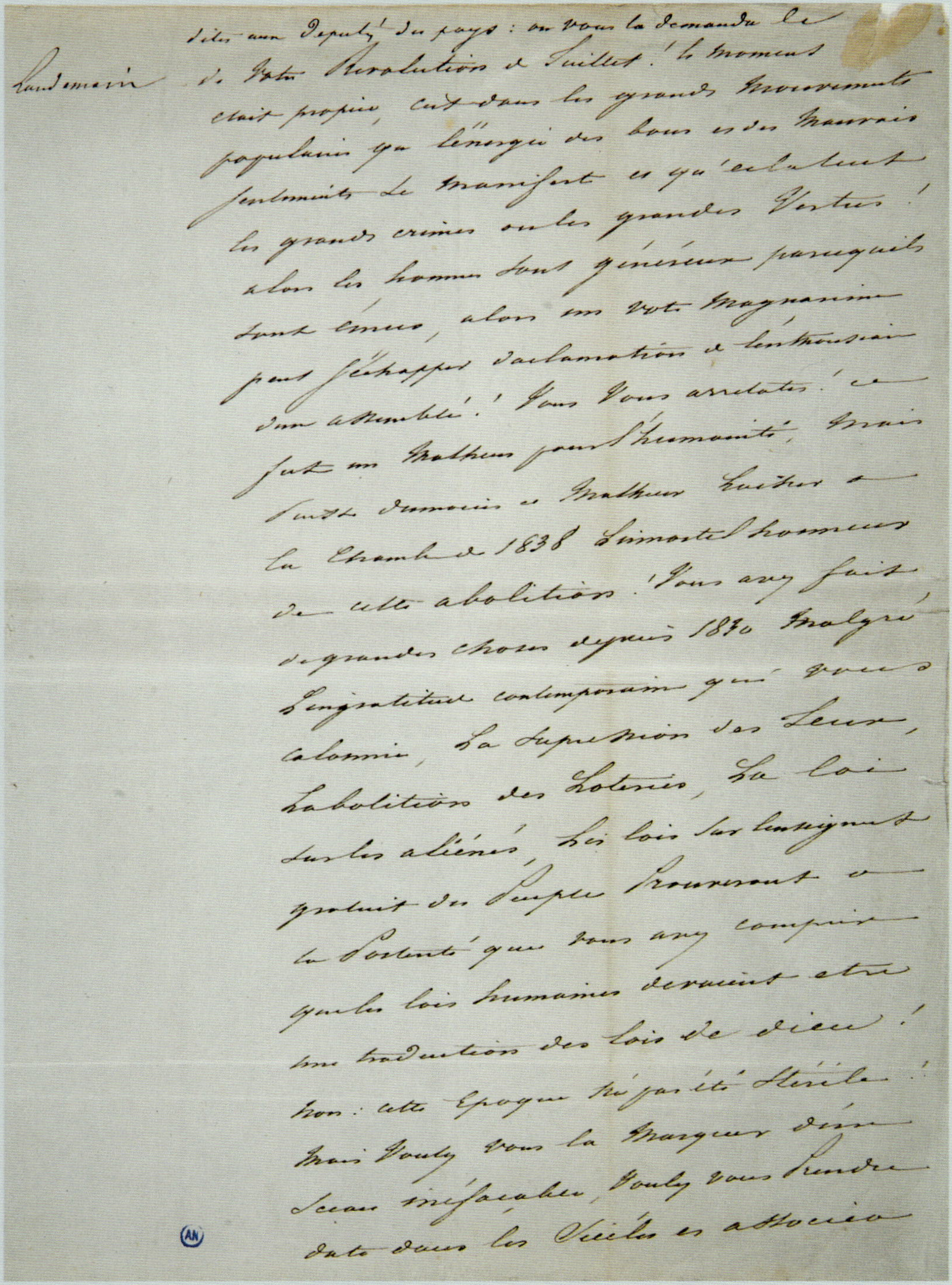
dites aux Députés du pays : on vous la demande le
lendemain de votre Révolution de Juillet ! le moment
était propice, c'est dans les grands mouvements
populaires que l'énergie des bons et des mauvais
sentiments se manifeste et qu'éclatent
les grands crimes ou les grandes vertus !
alors les hommes sont généreux parce qu'ils
sont émus, alors un vote magnanime
peut s'échapper d'acclamation et d'enthousiasme
d'une assemblée ! Vous vous arrêtâtes ! ce
fut un malheur pour l'humanité, mais
faites demain à ce malheur [illegible] à
la Chambre de 1838 l'immortel honneur
de cette abolition ! Vous avez fait
de grandes choses depuis 1830 malgré
l'ingratitude contemporaine qui vous
calomnie, la suppression des jeux,
l'abolition des loteries, la loi
sur les aliénés, les lois sur l'enseignement
gratuit du peuple prouveront à
la postérité que vous avez compris
que les lois humaines devaient être
une traduction des lois de Dieu !
Non : cette époque n'a pas été stérile !
mais voulez-vous la marquer d'un
sceau ineffaçable, voulez-vous rendre
datée dans les siècles et associée

ABOVE
Caricature of Lamartine
By Cham in *L'Assemblée nationale comique*.

LEFT
Lamartine against the death penalty
Parts of a speech. Around 1838, 1 page, in-4.

Alphonse de Lamartine (1790-1869), M.P. from 1833 to 1851, speaks in favour of the abolition of the death penalty: "Say to the representatives of this country: we asked it of you after your July Revolution! The moment was propitious... men can be generous in the midst of emotion...You did not pursue! This was a tragedy for Humanity but may this tragedy permit this Chamber tomorrow in 1838 to take the immortal and honorable step of abolishing! Replace the death penalty with life imprisonment and replace the notion of punishment with the idea of correction."

ABOVE

Caricature of Victor Hugo – The representatives represented

By Daumier in *Le Charivari*, July 20, 1849.

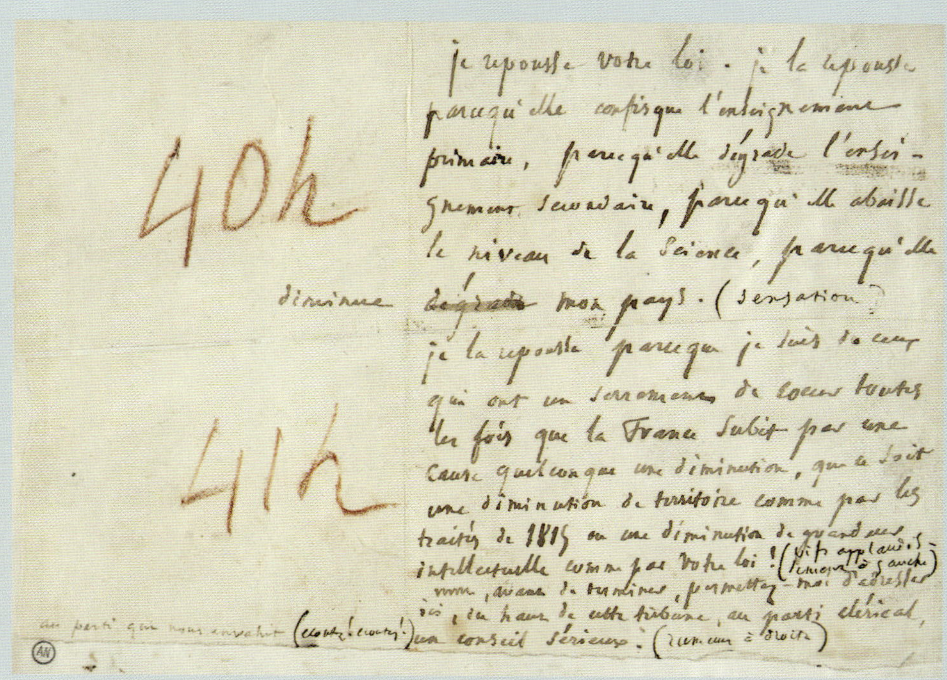
40h

41h

je repousse votre loi. je la repousse parcequ'elle confisque l'enseignement primaire, parcequ'elle dégrade l'enseignement secondaire, parcequ'elle abaisse le niveau de la science, parcequ'elle dégrade diminue mon pays. (sensation)

je la repousse parceque je suis de ceux qui ont un serrement de coeur toutes les fois que la France subit par une cause quelconque une diminution, que ce soit une diminution de territoire comme par les traités de 1815 ou une diminution de grandeur intellectuelle comme par votre loi ! (vifs applaudissements à gauche) ... du haut de cette tribune, au parti clérical, un conseil sérieux. (rumeurs à droite)

ABOVE RIGHT

Victor Hugo and education

Speech on the freedom of education made by Victor Hugo before the Legislative Assembly , 1850. Manuscript, 28 pages, in-8.

Victor Hugo (1802 - 1885), M.P. from 1848 to 1851, opposes the presence of the clergy on the supervisory boards of the public education system: " As far as I am concerned, we must maintain... this old and healthy separation between the Church and the State and I repeat it here that I seek what our fathers sought...that the Church remains within its domain and the State within its".

ABOVE

Georges Clemenceau, President of the Council and Minister for War, at the podium, November 11, 1918

In *L'Illustration*, November 16-23 , 1918.

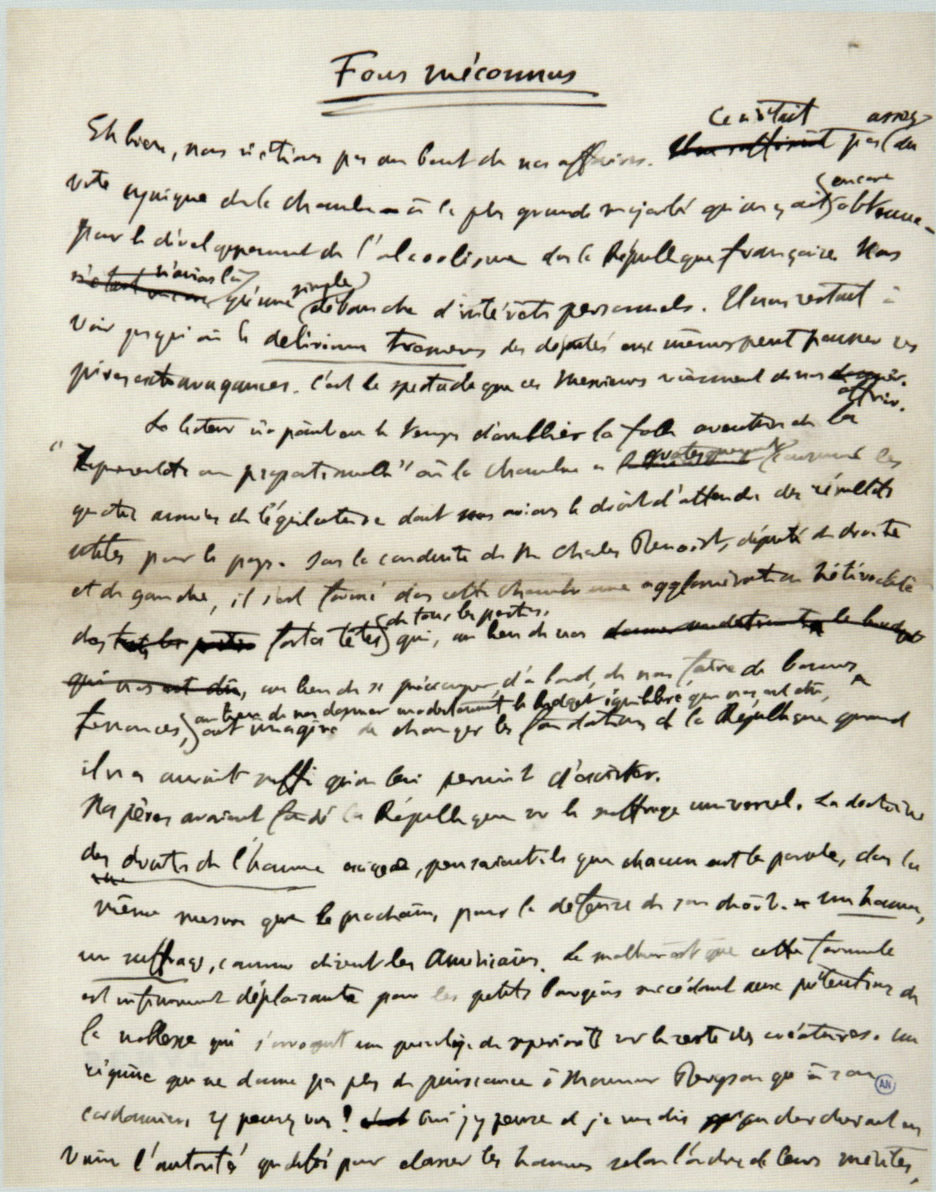
Fous méconnus

BELOW RIGHT

Clemenceau against the idea of proportional representation

Manuscript of a column in *L'Homme libre*, Georges Clemenceau. Around1913. 5 pages, in-4.

Clemenceau (1841–1929), M.P. from 1871 to 1893, attacks the principle of proportional representation: "Our fathers founded the Republic on the basis of universal suffrage...one man, one vote, as the Americans put it. The unfortunate thing is that such an idea is particularly offensive for the petty bourgeois classes...a regime which does not grant more influence to Mr Bergson than to his cobbler, can you imagine that? I can imagine it..."

THE CENTENARY OF A HUMANIST

Jaurès, the orator

ELECTED MEMBER of Parliament for the first time in 1885 at 26 years of age, Jean Jaurès (1859-1914) was one of the greatest orators of parliamentary history. He began his career as a moderate Republican but became the main actor in the unification of the workers' movement. The manuscripts held by the Library reflect the commitment of this great humanist. In this perspective, Jean Jaurès, in the huge introduction to his *Discours parlementaires*, "Parliamentary Speeches", reminds us of his convictions: "universal suffrage, despites its uncertainties and despite its surprises, is the light, the true light of day. Through it, all bodies are obliged to express their opinions, every thinking person is obliged to say what he has on his mind". This precious document was kept by the publisher Édouard Cornély, and was presented by Cornély's widow to Léon Blum to be bequeathed to the Library of the Chamber of Deputies where it has been conserved since 1931. Another manuscript, acquired by the Library in 1997 deals with the relations between the Radicals and the Socialists after the Radical Congress of Nancy. In it, Jaurès is very wary of the influence of the conservative wing of the Radical Party: "All we need to bear in mind is that on no occasion has our deep solidarity with the international proletariat and our unflinching wish to maintain peace, weakened our desire for national independence… Words mean nothing. Only action counts and we expect action. Or to go further, democracy expects action."

RIGHT HAND PAGE
Parliamentary speeches – Introduction: socialism and radicalism in 1885
1904. Manuscript, signed and dated by the author, 518 pages.

BELOW LEFT
Par les œuvres
Manuscript, signed by the author and written in November, 1907, 19 pages.

BELOW RIGHT
Jaurès at the podium in the Chamber of Deputies
[Detail]
By René Rousseau-Decelle, 1907.

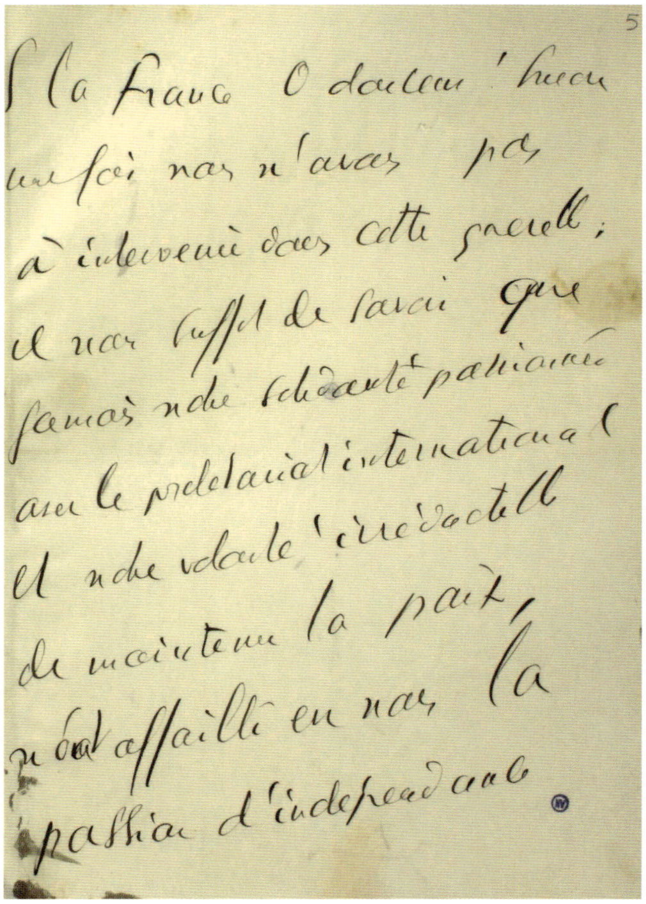

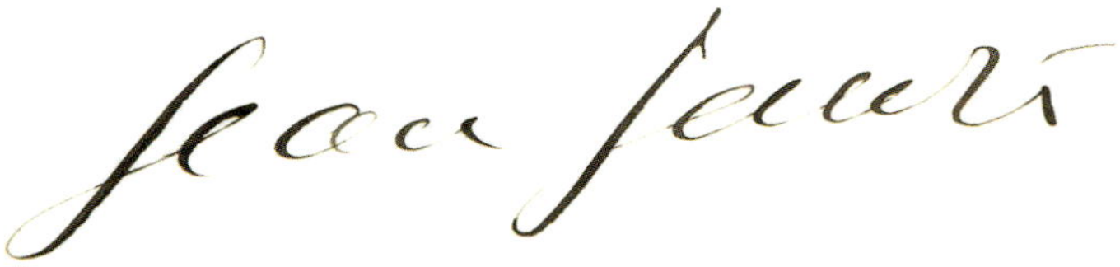

1145 lignes — gr. caps. 103

Introduction

~~Le socialisme et le radicalisme en 1885~~ Le socialisme et le radicalisme en 1885

J'ai cédé sans scrupule aux conseils de ceux qui me demandaient de réunir en volume mes discours parlementaires. Qu'on ne voie là ni péché d'orgueil ni faiblesse de vanité. L'homme politique qui mêlé à d'incessants combats s'attarderait avec ~~une~~ quelque ~~sorte de~~ complaisance littéraire à l'expression oratoire des luttes passées, serait bien frivole. Rien au demeurant ne fait ~~mieux~~ ressortir que ces sortes de publications la disproportion entre la force des événements et l'infinité de l'action individuelle. Mais il ne me paraît pas inutile de réunir quelques éléments de propagande qui peut-être seront utilisés par les militants socialistes et d'aider la démocratie toute entière à se faire une idée plus forte de la vérité ~~du parti~~ et de l'action de notre parti. Il ne me paraît pas inutile non plus en ce qui me concerne de marquer par des témoignages authentiques et irrécusables la ligne de développement que j'ai

Treasures and curiosities

Bringing together the spirit of the Enlightenment with a true love of books, the first two librarians, Camus and Druon, thought of the collection as a real "cabinet of curiosities" with its rare artifacts. The nave, which houses, amongst other treasures, the complete collection of the* Description de l'Égypte, *(the Description of Egypt) is the perfect example of this. However it is down in the strong-room where one can find several generations of encyclopedias, atlases and travel diaries that one can feel the truly insatiable appetite for learning.

The *Description de l'Égypte*

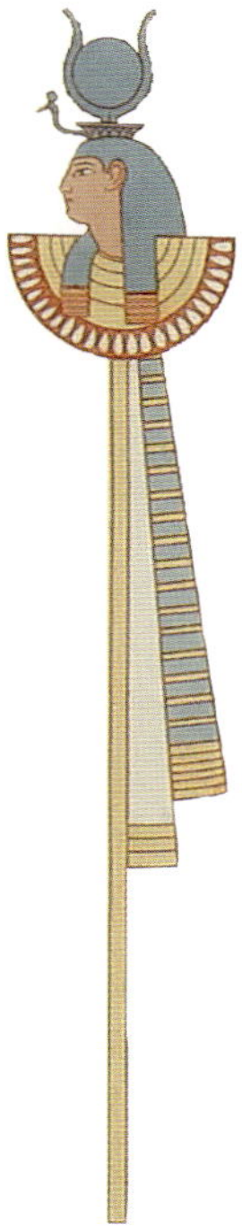

THE EXPEDITION WHICH LEFT TOULON in May 1798, led by Bonaparte included a host of scholars: the chemist Berthollet, the mathematician Monge, the mineralogist Dolomieu, the naturalist Geoffroy Saint-Hilaire, along with engineers and expert/graduates of France's elite science university the *École Polytechnique*. Led by Monge, who was to head the new Institute of Egypt in Cairo, these scholars set about studying archeology, the crafts and the living species which they encountered. Thus, they discovered, in Rosetta, a huge stone, of more than seven hundred kilogrammes which would open the road towards the decoding of hieroglyphics. After the resounding French military defeat, the scientists threatened to burn the results of their

LEFT HAND PAGE, FROM LEFT TO RIGHT, FROM TOP TO BOTTOM

Armillary sphere
xv^th^ Century.

Diary of Francisco Roïs
xvi^th^ Century.

OEdipus Aegyptiacus
Atanase Kircher
1652-1654.

Les Roses
Pierre-Joseph Redouté
1817-1821.

Description de l'Égypte
(The Description of Egypt)
1809-1828.

Voyage to Southern Russia and the Crimea
Anatolii Nicolaïevich Demidov
1842.

RIGHT

Description de l'Égypte
(The Description of Egypt)
Paris, 1809-1828. 9 volumes in-folio of texts and 14 albums in-plano of plates.

A collection of the observations and research carried out in Egypt under the leadership of Vivant Denon during the French Army's expedition.

work which the victorious English demanded to possess. In the end they did not take this step but had all their discoveries confiscated including the famous Rosetta Stone. However they did manage to make a copy and were able to pass it on to Jean-François Champollion. In 1802, Napoleon requested the publication, by the Imperial Print Works, of the scientific observations gathered during the expedition. This was to become the "Description of Egypt" which was to mobilize four hundred leather engravers over almost twenty years. This collection is made up of twenty-three volumes. Three of these volumes are cartographic and the size of the maps (over one metre) required the creation of special machines. The collection includes more than three thousand plates and one thousand copies were printed for its first edition. The piece of furniture in which it is housed in the Library is in the shape of an Egyptian pylon veneered in sycamore and bird's-eye maple in-laid with patterns in mahogany. It was built in 1837 by Haumont, the cabinet-maker of the Chamber of Deputies, upon the request of the *Questeurs*, the financial overseers of the Chamber.

LEFT AND TOP RIGHT
***Description de l'Égypte* (The Description of Egypt)**
Paris, 1809-1828. 9 volumes in-folio of texts and 14 albums in-plano of plates.

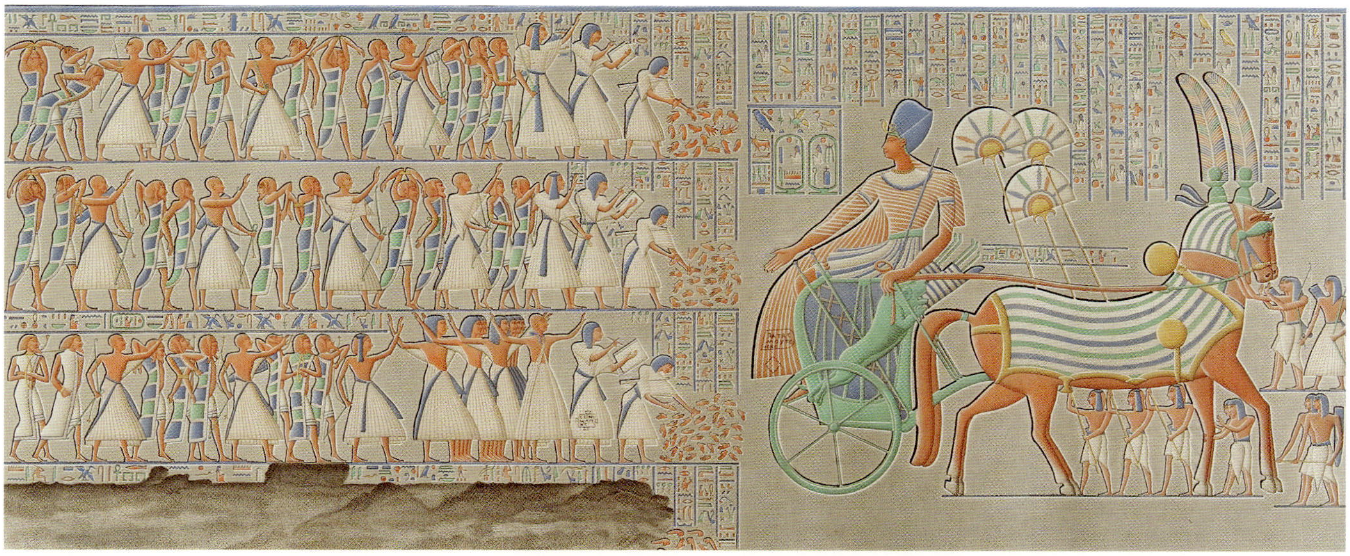

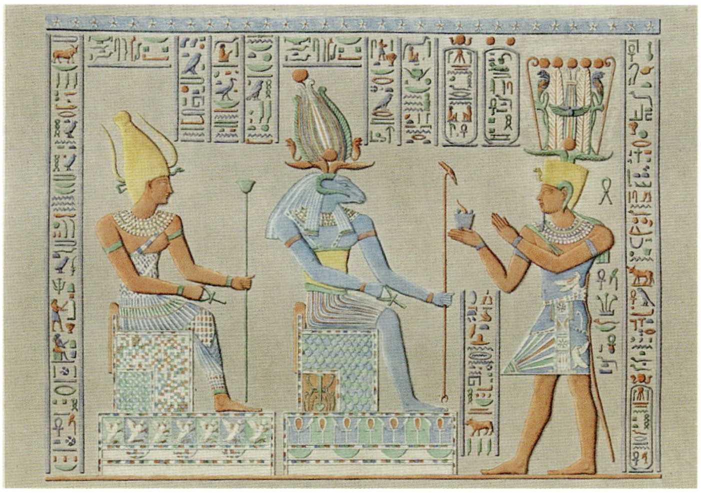

THE "MASTER OF A HUNDRED ARTS"

Atanase Kircher (1602-1680) was a German scientist, linguist and archeologist nicknamed the "Master of a Hundred Arts". He was the author of many works including this first true encyclopedia completely dedicated to Egypt. He attempted, in particular, to decipher hieroglyphics although he limited himself to a purely symbolic analysis.

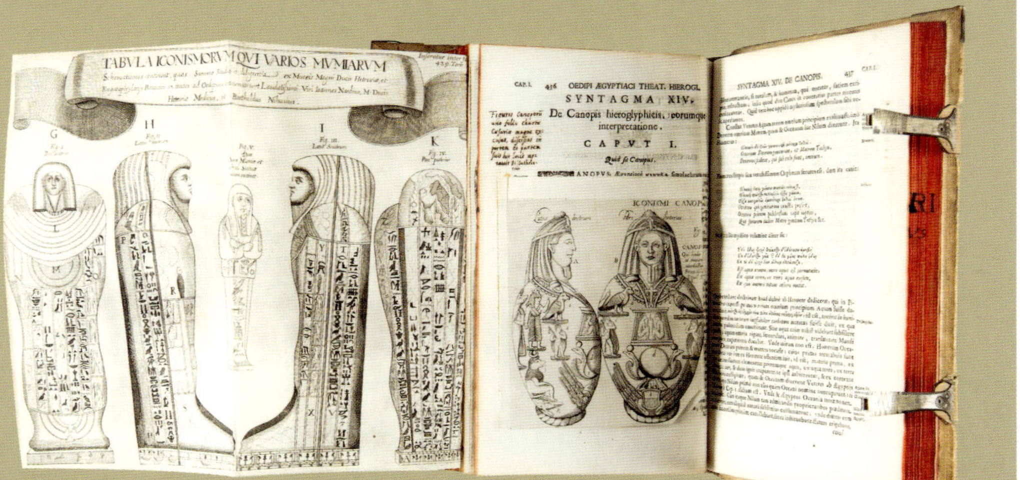

RIGHT
Œdipus Aegyptiacus
Atanase Kircher
Rome, Mascardi, 1652-1654.
3 parts in 2 volumes in-4, sow-skin binding on boards, blind-tooled designs in relief on the covers, spine with five raised bands, clasps.

Two hundred and fifty years of encyclopedias

ABOVE AND LEFT
The Chronicles of Nuremberg
Hartmann Schedel

Copy with colored illustrations, sow-skin binding on wooden boards.

This incunabulum was one of the most successful "best-sellers" in the early days of printing. The diversity and the size of its some one thousand eight hundred woodcuts make it the most richly illustrated work of its time. In this work, Hartmann Schedel, a German doctor and humanist, tells the story of humanity from its origins. He takes up Saint Augustin's notion of the six ages of the world and adds a seventh – the Last Judgment. The work also includes passages on natural catastrophes, portents and omens, wars, imperial or biblical genealogy as well as magnificent engravings of European towns.

RIGHT

Extensive Table of All the Liberal Arts
Christophe de Savigny

1619. Paris Libert, In-plano, binding in half-calfskin, spine with seven decorated raised bands.

This encyclopedia, which was ahead of its time, provides a summary table of the Arts. It was the work of the humanist scholar, Christophe de Savigny [1535?-1608?]. It defines learning in the shape of chains which represent a circle of knowledge within which each discipline has a very precise position. This copy is the second edition of the work which was first published in 1587.

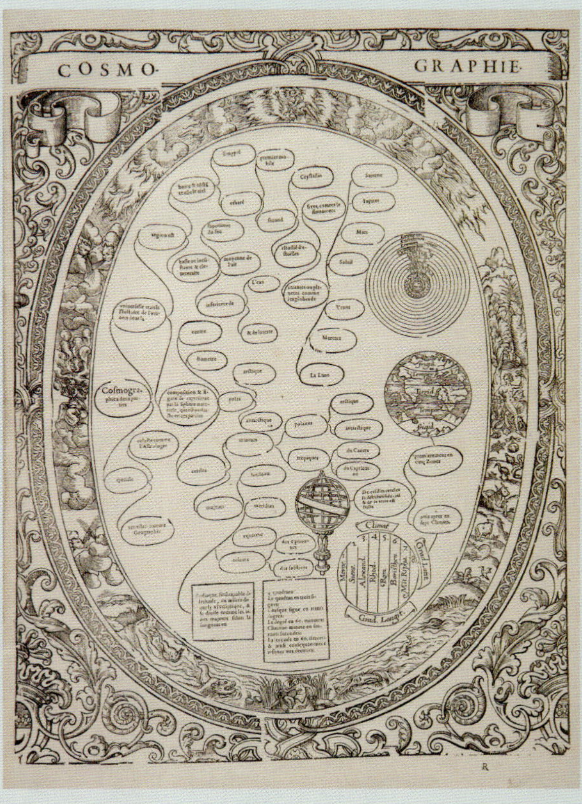

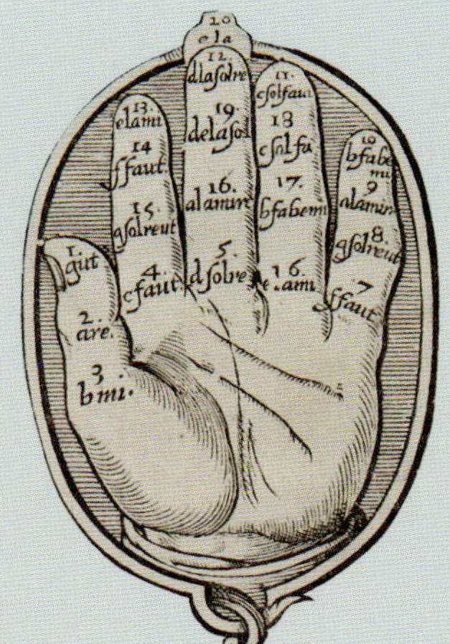

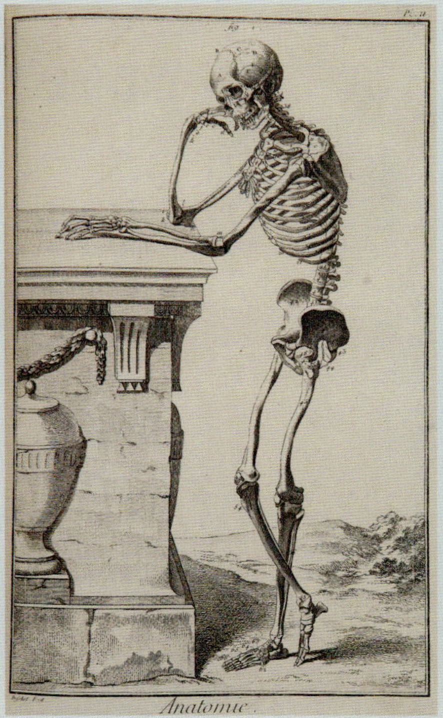

ABOVE FROM LEFT TO RIGHT

Cyclopoedia or An Universal Dictionary of Arts and Sciences
Ephraïm Chambers

London, 1751-1752. 2 volumes, in-folio.

Encyclopaedia, or a Systematic Dictionary of the Sciences, Arts, and Crafts by a Company of Men of Letters, arranged by M. Diderot and by M. d'Alembert

Paris, 1751. 35 volumes, in-folio, binding in speckled calfskin, spine with six decorated raised bands.

The two volumes of Ephraïm Chambers' [1680-1740] encyclopedia were published for the first time in London in 1728. Upon the request of various Parisian bookshop owners, the translation of this encyclopedia was entrusted to d'Alembert [1717-1783] and Diderot [1713-1784]. They provided the project with a totally different dimension. This was to be the birth of the *Systematic Dictionary of the Sciences, Arts, and Crafts*, which was the fruit of the labour of over one hundred and forty authors. This emblematic encyclopedia was illustrated with more than two thousand five hundred plates which are almost as famous as the *Encyclopédie* itself.

Perspectives on the world

ABOVE

***The Diary of Francisco Roïs followed by the Suma Oriental* by Tomé Pires**

1512-1520. Manuscripts, 178 and 124 pages.

The Diary is the work of one of the Captains of the fleet sent by the Governor of Portuguese India to discover the Moloccan Islands. Tomé Pires was the first European to head a diplomatic representation in Beijing. The *Suma Oriental* provides a description of the world from the Red Sea as far as China.

RIGHT

***A Natural History of Parrots* François Levaillant**

1801-1805, Paris. 2 volumes, in-folio, 145 plates.

This work, illustrated by the painter Jacques Barrabant, was published following the voyages of François Levaillant (1753-1824) to southern Africa. He brought back an impressive collection of parrots which he donated to the French Museum of Natural History.

RIGHT

Account of the Trip to South America Made in the Years 1712, 1713 and 1714, by Mr. Frezier, Simple Engineer of the King

1715. Manuscript dedicated to the King, 380 pages, binding in red Moroccan leather bearing the French coat of arms.

Amédée François Frezier [1687-1773] was an Engineering Officer who was sent by Louis XIV to observe the Spanish colonies in South America. He returned from his voyage with numerous maps of the coastline and plans of the harbours of Peru and Chile. He also brought back strawberry plants from Chile. These were presented to the Royal Garden and to the town of Plougastel on account of its propitious climate. After several crossing of plant species, the new variety of strawberry was to have the success that we all know today.

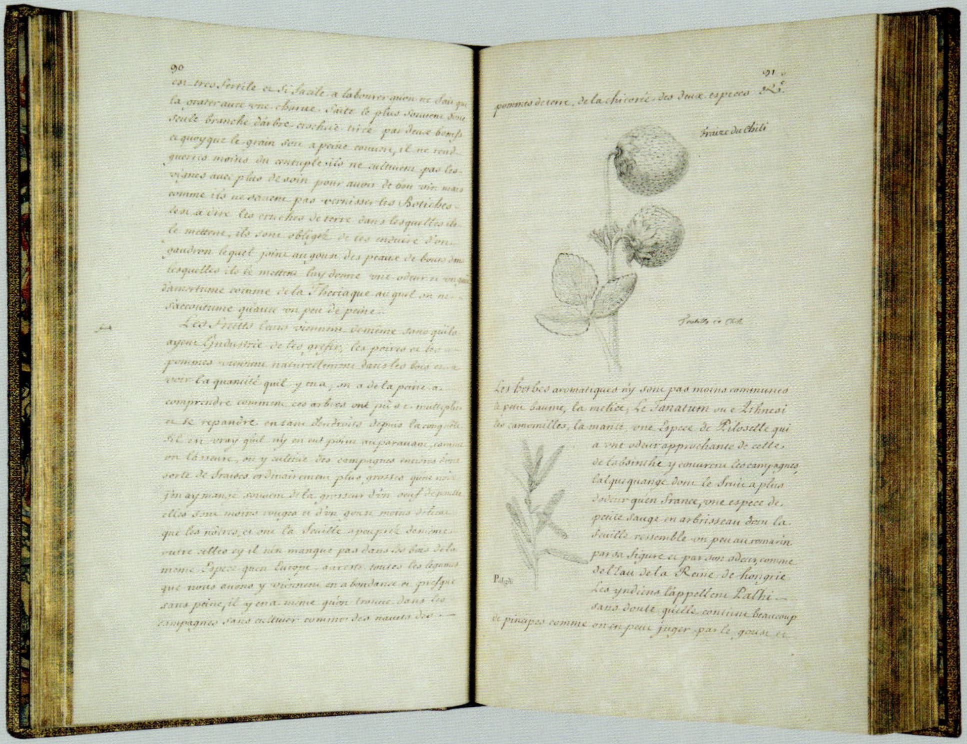

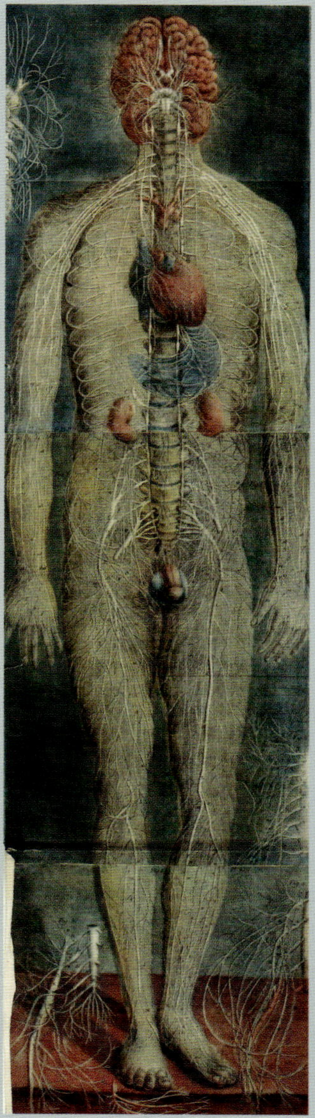

RIGHT

The Roses
Pierre-Joseph Redouté

1817-1821, Paris. 3 volumes in-folio, green half-calf binding. First edition.

Nicknamed the "Raphaël of flowers", Pierre-Joseph Redouté [1759-1840] was the official painter of Marie-Antoinette and then of Joséphine de Beauharnais before becoming the painting teacher of Marie-Louise de Habsbourg.

EXTREME RIGHT

Anatomy of Reproduction
Jacques Gautier Dagoty

1773, Paris. In-folio, green Moroccan leather with the Royal coat of arms. Original edition.

Jacques Gautier Dagoty [1710-1785] was a painter, engraver and physician who was the author of several anatomical studies.

Treasures
of literature

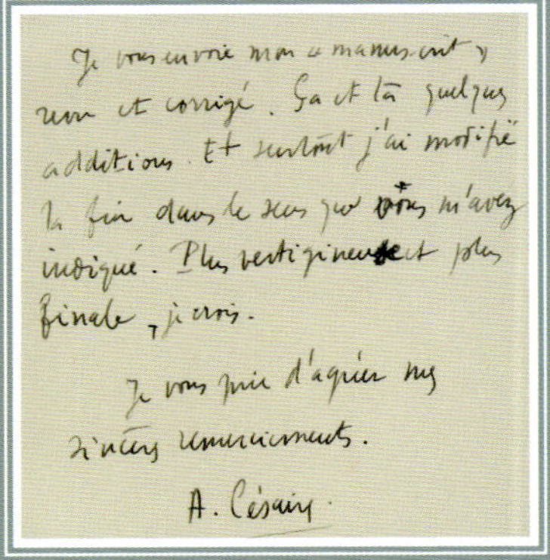
Je vous envoie mon manuscrit, revu et corrigé. Ça et là quelques additions. Et surtout j'ai modifié la fin dans le sens que vous m'avez indiqué. Plus vertigineusement folie finale, je crois.

Je vous prie d'agréer mes sincères remerciements.

A. Césaire

In addition to magnificent editions by Petrarch, La Bruyère, La Fontaine or Molière, the Library also possesses some ninety incunabula (works published before the XVIth Century) among which feature the famous "Roman de la rose". There are also priceless manuscripts by Jean-Jacques Rousseau, the pre-eminent figure in the run-up to the French Revolution who is today buried in the Panthéon and who through his works has entered the National Assembly.

Ovid's *Heroides*

DESPITE THE UNFORTUNATE FACT that it has been torn and damaged, this manuscript on vellum still contains fifteen beautiful paintings attributed to the illuminator, Jean Pichore. This classic work by the Latin poet Ovid (43 BC-17 AD) was translated in verse by the poet Octavien de Saint-Gelais who was also the Bishop of Angoulême. He dedicated his translation to Charles VIII. It is made up of twenty-one fictional letters exchanged between two characters from mythology. Only around ten similar manuscripts have been documented in France or in European libraries.

LEFT HAND PAGE, FROM LEFT TO RIGHT AND FROM TOP TO BOTTOM

The *Roman de la rose* Guillaume de Lorris and Jean de Meung
XIVth Century.

The Theatre of Molière
1734.

Shelves from the Library.

***Le Devin du village, "The Village Soothsayer"* Jean-Jacques Rousseau**
Around 1752.

The History of the French Royal Academy of Sciences
1788. Binding with the arms of *Philippe Égalité*.

***Cahier d'un retour au pays natal, "Notebook of a Return to my Native Land",* Aimé Césaire, M.P. for Martinique**
1939. Typed manuscript with annotations.

RIGHT

***The Heroides* (or the Epistles) Ovid**
XVIth Century. Manuscript, translation in French in verse.

A MASTERPIECE OF THE MIDDLE AGES

Le Roman de la rose

THIS WORK, which was extremely successful, is an allegorical poem of over twenty-two thousand verses and was written by two authors from the Middle Ages: Guillaume de Lorris, who began it around 1230 and Jean de Meung who finished it forty years later. This work, which was for a long time a subject of controversy, is both an ode to courtly love and a cynical analysis of the art of seduction. It also represents an encyclopedic collection of learning at that time. In the world there are some three hundred manuscripts from the XIIIth to the XVIth Centuries which have been identified and the Library possesses two copies of this "best-seller" from the Middle Ages: a manuscript which bears the effects of wear over time and of having been frequently handled, coming to us from the "literary stores" of the Revolution and an incunabulum on vellum, printed in 1497, which is illustrated by ninety-seven illuminated figures.

LEFT

The *Roman de la rose* Guillaume de Lorris and Jean de Meung

XIVth Century. Manuscript on parchment, 148 pages, 24 illustrations, binding in mottled calfskin.

LEFT HAND PAGE

The *Roman de la rose* Guillaume de Lorris and Jean de Meung

1497, Paris. Antoine Vérard, in-folio, binding in green Moroccan leather with a floral decoration and with a decorated ribbed spine.

Cy est le rommant de la rose
Ou tout lart damours est enclose.

Maintes gens dient q̄ en songes
Ne sont que fables & mẽsonges
Mais on peult telz songes songier
Qui ne sont mie mensongier
Ains sont apres bien apparant
Si en puis bien trouuer garant
Vng acteur denomme macrobes
Qui ne tient pas songes a lobes
Aincoys escript la vision
Qui aduint au roy cipion
Quiconques cuide ne qui die
Que ce soit vne musardie
De croire que songe aduiengne
Et qui vouldra pour fol mentiengne
Car endroit moy ay ie fiance
Que songe soit signifiance
Des biens aux gens & des ennuyz
Que les plusieurs songent par nuytz
Moult de choses couuertement
Que on voit puis appertement
Au vingtiesme an de mon eage
Ou point qu amours prent le peage
Des ieunes gens couchie mestoie
Vne nuyt comme ie souloye
Et me dormoye moult forment
Si vey vng songe en mon dormant
Qui moult fut bel a aduiser
Comme vous orrez deuiser
Car en aduisant moult me pleut
Mais en songes onques riens neut
Qui aduenu du tout ne soit
Comme listoire le recoit
Or vueil ce songe rimoyer
Pour voz cueurs plus fort esgayer
Amours le me prie & commande
Et se nulz ou nulle demande
Comment ie vueil que ce rommans
Soit appelle: que ie commans
Que cest le rommant de la rose
Ou lart damurs est toute enclose
La matiere en est bonne & briefue
Or doint dieu quen gre la recoyue
Celle pour qui ie lay enpris
Cest vne dame de hault pris
Et tant est digne destre amee
Quelle doit rose estre clamee
Aduis mestoit a ceste foys
Bien ay cinq ans & cinq moys
Que ou moys de may ie songoye
Ou temps amoureux plein de ioye
Quil ny a ne buissons ne haye
Qui en celluy temps ne sesgaye
Et en may parer ne se vueille
Et couurir de nouuelle fueille
Les boys recouurent leur verdure

A MODERN POLITICAL THINKER

The priceless Jean-Jacques Rousseau collection

THE MANUSCRIPTS of Jean-Jacques Rousseau were acquired by the National Assembly in a variety of ways. Some of them were given to the Convention, (*Confessions*, and the first draft of *Julie or the New Heloise*) others came from the collections confiscated at the time of the Revolution (two volumes of his personal copy of *Julie or the New Heloise* and the rough draft for *Emile* were impounded at the house of Hérault de Séchelles, who was guillotined in 1794. The six-volume copy of *Julie or the New Heloise* was presented by Rousseau to the Maréchale de Luxembourg and impounded after the latter emigrated in 1794). In addition, a manuscript version of the *Dialogues* of Jean-Jacques Rousseau, the music of *The Village Soothsayer*, as well as that of *La Botanique mise à la portée de tout le monde* by Messers and Madam Regnault, annotated in Rousseau's own hand, were acquired by Druon, the second custodian of the Library.

RIGHT HAND PAGE
Emile, or On Education
Jean-Jacques Rousseau
Personal copy. Autographed copy, 3 volumes, in-8, binding in red Moroccan leather.

EXTREME LEFT
La Nouvelle Héloïse, "Julie or the New Heloise"
Jean-Jacques Rousseau
1760. Copy for the Maréchale de Luxembourg. 6 volumes, each illustrated with original drawings by Gravelot.

RIGHT
Complete Works
Jean-Jacques Rousseau
1788-1793. 34 volumes.

de fripon public, l'autre celui de valet rampant avec ce beau mot, *il faut que je vive*. 61

Vous vous fiez à l'ordre actuel de la société, sans songer que cet ordre est sujet à des révolutions inévitables et qu'il vous est impossible de prévoir ni de prévenir celle qui peut regarder vos enfans. Le Grand devient petit, le riche devient pauvre, le monarque devient sujet: Les coups du sort sont-ils si rares que vous puissiez compter d'en être exempt? Tout ce qu'ont fait les hommes, les hommes peuvent le détruire. Il n'y a de caractéres inéfaçables que ceux qu'imprime la nature, et la nature ne fait ni princes, ni riches, ni grands seigneurs. Que fera donc dans la bassesse ce Satrape que vous n'avez élevé que pour la grandeur? Que fera dans la pauvreté ce publicain qui ne sait vivre que d'or? Que fera dépourvu de tout ce fastueux imbécille qui ne sait point user de lui-même et ne met son être que dans ce qui est étranger à lui? Heureux celui qui sait quiter alors l'état qui le quite et rester homme en dépit du sort. Qu'on loue tant qu'on voudra ~~un~~ ce Roi vaincu qui veut s'enterrer en furieux sous les débris de son trône; moi, je le méprise; je vois qu'il n'éxiste que par sa couronne et qu'il n'est rien du tout, s'il n'est Roi. Mais celui qui la perd et s'en passe est alors au dessus d'elle. Du rang de Roi qu'un lâche, un méchant un fou peut remplir comme un

61/2 autre || il monte à l'état d'homme que si peu d'hommes savent remplir. Alors, il

THE CONVENTION RECEIVES *LES CONFESSIONS*

The secrets behind a manuscript

IN HIS *CONFESSIONS*, written between 1765 and 1770, Jean-Jacques Rousseau, who was attacked from all sides, sets down reasons for his philosophy of life. The philosopher wrote three manuscripts which are very different from the *Confessions* which are held today in the libraries of Geneva, Neuchâtel and the *Palais-Bourbon*. The so-called "Paris" manuscript, made up of two volumes which Jean-Jacques Rousseau kept with him, were handed over to the National Convention on September 26, 1794, sixteen years after the death of the philosopher, by his widow, Thérèse Levasseur. Written on the two envelopes, each of which contained one of these volumes that had been closed with the seal of Jean-Jacques Rousseau, were the instructions, written before the death of the author, clearly stating that they were not to be opened before 1801. It was decided to open them and to entrust the contents to Lakanal, so as to protect, during their lifetime, the persons who were mentioned. This was done, in the same way that the great man's ashes were conserved in the Panthéon, in order to immortalize his work. The French Republic, with this vote by the Convention, set itself up as the legitimate heir of Rousseau. In 1798, the Council of the Five Hundred decided that the manuscript should be placed in the archives of the Legislative body.

BELOW AND RIGHT
Les Confessions
Jean-Jacques Rousseau
Manuscript containing two volumes of 182 and 172 pages, in-12, soft back, covered with floral paper and a parchment spine, in a red Moroccan leather case.

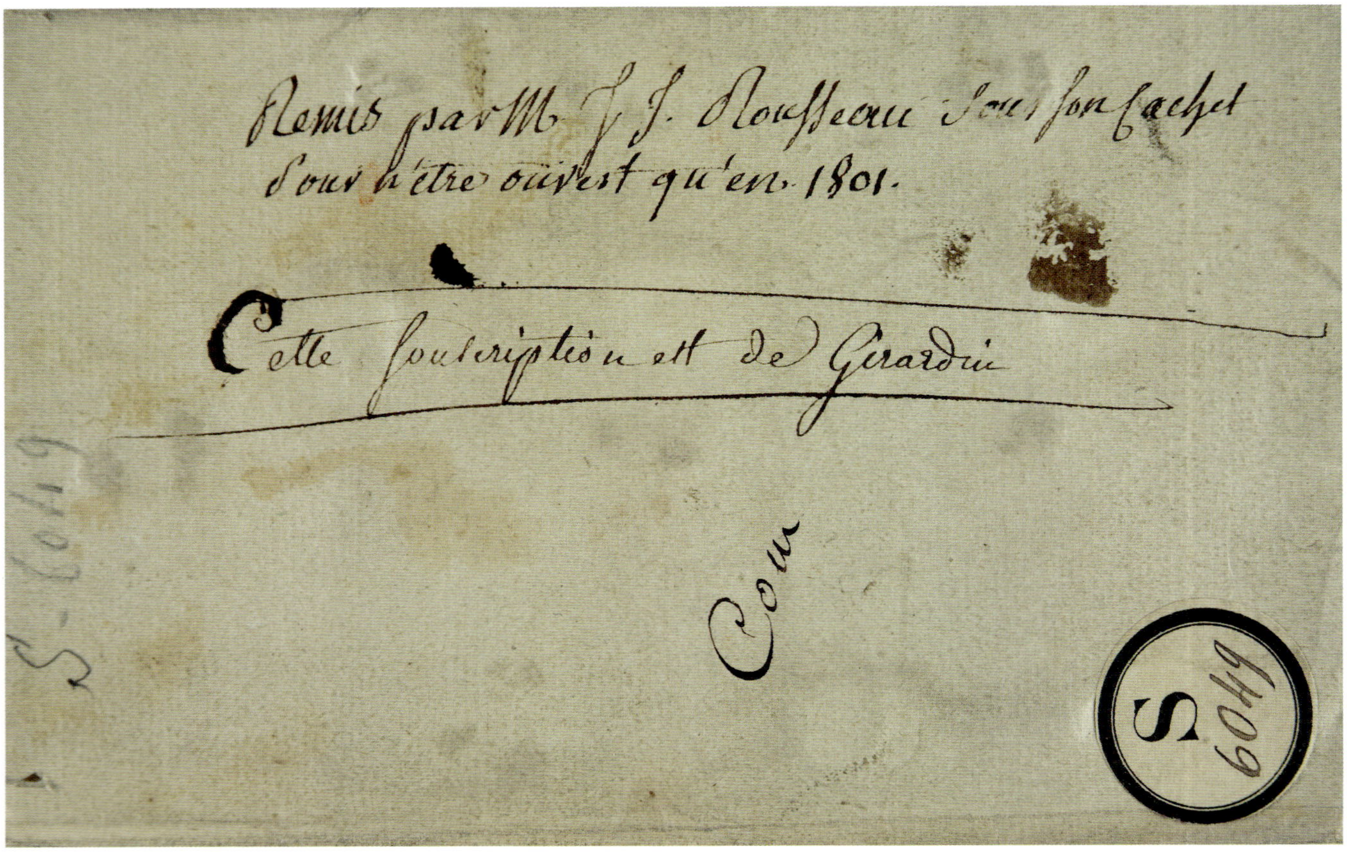

de fripon public, l'autre celui de valet rampant 61
avec ce beau mot, <u>il faut que je vive.</u>

Vous vous fiez à l'ordre actuel de la société, sans songer
que cet ordre est sujet à des révolutions
inévitables et qu'il vous est impossible de
prévoir ni de prévenir celle qui peut regarder
vos enfans. Le Grand devient petit, le riche
devient pauvre, le monarque devient sujet: Les
coups du sort sont-ils si rares que vous puissiez
compter d'en être exempt? Tout ce qu'ont fait
les hommes, les hommes peuvent le détruire. Il n'y
a de caractéres inéfaçables que ceux qu'imprime
la nature, et la nature ne fait ni princes, ni
riches, ni grands seigneurs. Que fera donc
dans la bassesse ce Satrape que vous n'avez
elevé que pour la grandeur? Que fera dans
la pauvreté ce publicain qui ne sait vivre
que d'or? Que fera dépourvu de tout ce
fastueux imbécille qui ne sait point user de
lui-même et ne met son être que dans ce
qui est étranger à lui? Heureux celui qui
sait quiter alors l'état qui le quite et rester
homme en dépit du sort. Qu'on loüe tant
qu'on voudra ~~un~~ ce Roi vaincu qui veut
s'enterrer en furieux sous les débris de son
trône; moi, je le méprise; je vois qu'il
n'existe que par sa couronne et qu'il n'est
rien du tout, s'il n'est Roi. Mais celui qui
la perd et s'en passe est alors au dessus
d'elle. Du rang de Roi qu'un lâche, un
méchant un fou peut remplir comme un
81 / 2 autre // il monte à l'état d'homme que si
peu d'hommes savent remplir. Alors, il

THE CONVENTION RECEIVES *LES CONFESSIONS*

The secrets behind a manuscript

IN HIS *CONFESSIONS*, written between 1765 and 1770, Jean-Jacques Rousseau, who was attacked from all sides, sets down reasons for his philosophy of life. The philosopher wrote three manuscripts which are very different from the *Confessions* which are held today in the libraries of Geneva, Neuchâtel and the *Palais-Bourbon*. The so-called "Paris" manuscript, made up of two volumes which Jean-Jacques Rousseau kept with him, were handed over to the National Convention on September 26, 1794, sixteen years after the death of the philosopher, by his widow, Thérèse Levasseur. Written on the two envelopes, each of which contained one of these volumes that had been closed with the seal of Jean-Jacques Rousseau, were the instructions, written before the death of the author, clearly stating that they were not to be opened before 1801. It was decided to open them and to entrust the contents to Lakanal, so as to protect, during their lifetime, the persons who were mentioned. This was done, in the same way that the great man's ashes were conserved in the Panthéon, in order to immortalize his work. The French Republic, with this vote by the Convention, set itself up as the legitimate heir of Rousseau. In 1798, the Council of the Five Hundred decided that the manuscript should be placed in the archives of the Legislative body.

BELOW AND RIGHT
Les Confessions
Jean-Jacques Rousseau
Manuscript containing two volumes of 182 and 172 pages, in-12, soft back, covered with floral paper and a parchment spine, in a red Moroccan leather case.

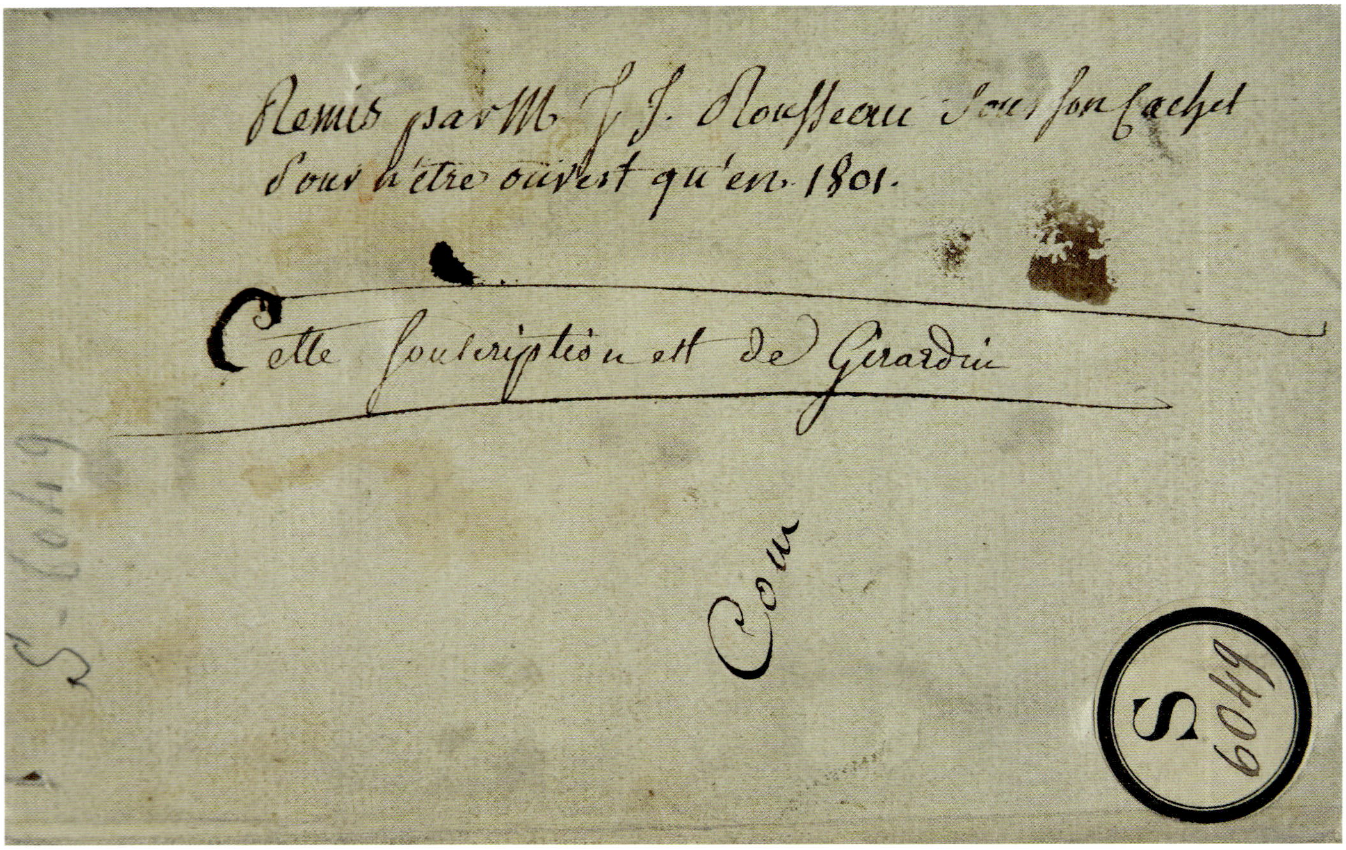

(I) Les Confessions de J. J. Rousseau. J. Bozier[sic] — L. Souhet
Prémiére Partie. ne Sanseur fre
Rozeau Livre I. Lasorte Barbeau dubarran
Cordier, Intùs et in Cute. Pelet, fre — ex-président
gere pag.

1. Je forme une entreprise qui n'eut jamais d'exemple, et qui n'aura point d'imitateur. Je veux montrer à mes semblables un homme dans toute la vérité de la nature, et cet homme, ce sera moi.

2. Moi seul. Je sens mon coeur, et je connois les hommes. Je ne suis fait comme aucun de ceux que j'ai vus; j'ose croire n'être fait comme aucun de ceux qui existent. Si je ne vaux pas mieux, au moins je suis autre. Si la nature a bien ou mal fait de briser le moule dans lequel elle m'a jetté, c'est ce dont on ne peut juger qu'après m'avoir lû.

3. Que la trompette du jugement dernier sonne quand elle voudra. Je viendrai ce livre à la main me présenter devant le Souverain juge. Je dirai hautement: voila ce que j'ai fait, ce que j'ai pensé, ce que je fus. J'ai dit le bien et le mal avec la même franchise. Je n'ai rien tu de mauvais, rien ajouté de bon, et s'il m'est arrivé d'employer quelque ornement indifférent, ce n'a jamais été que pour remplir un vide occasionné par mon défaut de mémoire; j'ai pu supposer vrai ce que je savois avoir pu l'être, jamais ce que je savois être faux. Je me suis montré tel que je fus, méprisable et vil quand je l'ai été, bon généreux sublime quand je l'ai été: j'ai dévoilé mon intérieur tel que tu l'as vu toi-même. Etre éternel, rassemble autour de moi l'innombrable foule de mes semblables: qu'ils écoutent mes confessions, X qu'ils gémissent de mes miséres. Que chacun d'eux découvre à son tour son coeur aux pieds de ton trone; et puis qu'un seul te dise, s'il l'ose: Je fus meilleur que cet homme-là.

\# avec la même sincerité

X qu'ils rougissent de mes indignités,

2. 1. Je suis né à Genève en 1712 d'Isaac Rousseau Citoyen et de Susanne Bernard Citoyenne. Un bien fort médiocre à partager entre quinze enfans ayant réduit presque à rien la portion de mon pere, il n'avoit pour subsister que son métier d'horloger, dans lequel il étoit à la vérité fort habile. Ma mere, fille du ministre Bernard étoit plus riche elle avoit de la sagesse et de la beauté: ce n'étoit pas sans peine que mon pere l'avoit obtenue. Leurs amours avoient commencé presque avec leur vie: dès l'âge de huit à neuf ans ils se promenoient ensemble tous les soirs sur la Treille; à dix ans ils ne pouvoient plus se quitter. La simpathie, l'accord des ames affermit en eux le sentiment qu'avoit produit l'habitude. Tous deux, nés tendres et sensibles, n'attendoient que le moment de trouver dans un autre la même disposition ou plustot ce moment les attendoit eux-mêmes, et chacun d'eux jetta son coeur dans le premier qui s'ouvrit pour le recevoir. Le sort qui sembloit contrarier leur passion ne fit que l'animer. Le jeune amant ne pouvant obtenir sa maitresse se consumoit de douleur; elle lui conseilla de voyager pour l'oublier. Il voyagea sans fruit et revint plus amoureux que jamais. Il retrouva celle qu'il aimoit tendre et fidelle. Après cette épreuve il ne restoit qu'à s'aimer toute la vie; ils le jurérent, et le ciel bénit leur serment.

2. Gabriel Bernard frére de ma mére devint amoureux d'une des soeurs de mon pere; mais elle ne consentit à epouser le frére qu'à condition que son frére epouseroit la soeur. L'amour arrangea tout et les deux mariages se firent le même jour. Ainsi mon oncle étoit le mari de ma tante, et leurs enfans furent doublement mes cousins germains. Il en naquit un de part et d'autre au bout d'une année; ensuite il fallut encore se séparer.

3. Mon Oncle Bernard étoit Ingénieur. Il alla servir dans l'empire et en hongrie sous le Prince Eugène. Il se distinga au siége et à la bataille de Belgrade. Mon pere, après la naissance de mon frére unique partit pour Constantinople où il étoit appellé, et devint horloger du serrail. Durant son absence, la beauté de ma mere, son esprit, ses talens* lui attirérent des hommages. M. de la Closure

*Elle en avoit de trop brillans pour son état, le Ministre son pere

THE NATIONAL ASSEMBLY OPENS ITS DOORS TO YOU

ASSEMBLÉE NATIONALE

VISITING THE NATIONAL ASSEMBLY AND ITS LIBRARY

All information concerning visits of the National Assembly (times, reservation, and access) is available on the internet site:

www.assemblee-nationale.fr
at the section « Découvrir l'Assemblée ».

You can find digitized versions of the works from the collection of the Library at « Découvrir l'Assemblée/Patrimoine ».
You can also find up-to-date information (live debates and on-request videos, M.P.s' profiles, committee proceedings and parliamentary documents etc.) on the same internet site as well as on the Twitter account and the Facebook and Google+ pages of the National Assembly.

THE BOUTIQUE OF THE NATIONAL ASSEMBLY

To remember your visit: 7, rue Aristide-Briand 75007 Paris
And on internet: boutique.assemblee-nationale.fr

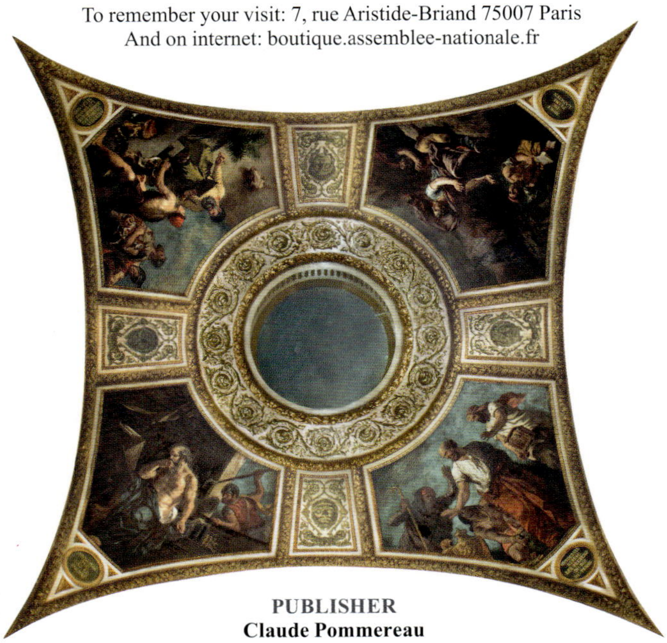

PUBLISHER
Claude Pommereau

EDITOR IN CHIEF
Rafael Pic

ARTISTIC DIRECTOR
Bernard Borel

GRAPHIC DESIGN
Julie Linotte

ICONOGRAPHER
Florelle Guillaume

EDITING SECRETARY
Virginie Vernevaut

ENGLISH TRANSLATION
Declan Mc Cavana

TTM ÉDITIONS / BEAUX ARTS ÉDITIONS

Photogravure Key Graphic, Paris

Printed in France
Dépôt légal August 2014
ISBN Beaux-Arts éditions 979-1-02040-109-0

THE PUBLISHER THANKS:
The departments of the National Assembly:

The Library and Archives Department of the National Assembly and the Communication, Information and Multimedia Department

Cover: ***The Library of the National Assembly***
Overview. The ceiling, 1838-1847, by Eugène Delacroix.
Palais-Bourbon.

Above: ***The Dome of Sciences***
by Delacroix.

Opposite page:
The Tennis Court Oath
Signatures of M.P.s who voted for the oath, June 20, 1789.

Back cover: ***The Dome of Poetry,***
Alexander and the poems of Homer
by Delacroix.